INSIDE THE METAVERSE

What the Metaverse Is and How Virtual Worlds and Digital Economies Work

Arkon Flux

TABLE OF CONTENTS

ISBN: 9781807651121

Published by TPSA Publishing

INTRODUCTION

Not ten years ago, if someone had mentioned that our money would some day turn completely digital, nobody would have believed them. Nowadays, however, this idea does not seem quite so implausible. Words such as "bitcoin," "blockchain," and "NFT" seem to be spreading around the Internet at an alarmingly accelerating pace. In fact, now more than ever, it is of vital importance to get on board with this new digital currency system as the world has found itself at a complete shifting point between the physical and digital.

In the fall of 2021, Mark Zuckerberg announced a rebrand of his multi-billion-dollar company, Facebook, into something called "Meta." This alludes to a long-term project which he has in the works: the *metaverse*, an online avatar platform that will bring humanity ever closer to a complete digital immersion experience. To this end, it has been made clear that this may very well be the top investment opportunity of the century.

What is Cryptocurrency?

The term "cryptocurrency" is thrown around loosely. It is usually most strongly associated with the idea of Bitcoin, which is, as the name itself states, a coin that exists solely in bits, a measure of storage on a computer. However, Bitcoin is in fact just one of many—over 4,000—different types of cryptocurrencies. Each of these are encoded with slightly different algorithms, branded differently, and kept by different ledgers in blockchains. As an investor, it is your job to decide how to split your money between the most favorable cryptocurrencies in order to profit from the continuously growing online market.

Digital Currency

The idea behind cryptocurrency is still fairly new, and can be summed up by the words "digital currency." The first inkling of digital money was in the late 1980s, where the desire for an untraceable, decentralized currency system became more and more apparent, however nothing was truly produced until the 1990s. The crypto that we know today is slightly different from this idea, not being completely untraceable, but it remains decentralized and maintained by a peer-to-peer (P2P) system which will be discussed further in Chapter 1. These reasons along with the secure and non-physical nature of the product have been the main driving forces for people to buy and sell products with the use of bitcoins or similar currencies.

Non-Fungible Tokens (NFTs)

Relating to cryptocurrency, there is the ever-growing market for non-fungible tokens, or NFTs, which is essentially the act of buying and selling of ownership over an art piece, which can be as simple as a jpeg file and worth as much as $69 million, as is the case with a certain picture, called 'Everydays - The First 5000 Days' by Beeple (Kastrenakes, 2021). The purchase of NFTs is a controversial topic, as some people do not understand the value in buying simply a part of the ownership of a picture without any rights to it, however this does not change the fact that the market for them is booming and there is money to be made in it.

The Metaverse

The metaverse, as previously mentioned, represents Mark Zuckerberg's vision for the future of the Internet, however he is not the only one with these goals. Many other companies—including large ones such as Microsoft—also seek to monopolize this project, and therefore it is no longer purely being developed by one organization. In the future, the metaverse seeks to be an immersive online experience, similar to some video games already on the market like Minecraft, Fortnite, or Roblox, for which, by the success that these mega-games have seen, there is an exorbitant demand.

Augmented Reality

One of the main principles on which the idea of the metaverse is based is that of augmented reality. At its core, augmented reality is to take the real world and add extra visual, auditory, and sensory elements to it. Thus, the metaverse aims to augment our reality. AR is different from a similar concept, virtual reality (VR), in that VR completely transforms reality, transporting the user to a different world. AR, in contrast, takes the real world and adds information to it. More elaboration on this topic will come from Chapter 4.

A Note from the Author

Antony Shen has been an avid crypto investor ever since he first put money into Bitcoin in 2016. Since then, he has learned the ins and outs of cryptocurrency investment through trial and error. Ultimately, Shen discovered some core strategies and tactics to invest wisely for maximum profit. In this book, he will start from the basics and explain the depths of cryptocurrency and its inner-workings from a technological standpoint. He will elaborate on the reason people gravitate towards this new method of "banking" and transaction. Then, you will move on to more complicated topics, such as the purchasing of NFTs, the idea of non-fungible tokens, as you may recall, the implementation of augmented reality and associated hardware, and finally the concept of blockchain gaming, where people may be able to earn cryptocurrency by playing a videogame wired to the blockchain.

After having conceptualized all these terms, you will move on to learn everything there is to know, up to date, about the long-term project that has been all over the news: the metaverse. You will come to understand how all these cryptocurrency notions will be implemented and enhanced through the metaverse platforms and thus why it is such a revolutionary topic—one that is garnering mass interest. Through this, you will fully understand why the metaverse is such a golden opportunity for investment.

Finally, you will begin to learn how you can get started with crypto investing. You will learn strategies to choose how much money to spend, how to divide your investments to cover your bases, and how to choose where to divide them. You will learn how to make money from NFTs, either as an artist or an investor, as well as how to profit from blockchain gaming and AR opportunities. After having all the knowledge of these already well-established investment areas under your belt, you will bring it all together through the numerous metaverse projects, fully understanding the risks and rewards associated with this kind of passive income. You will come out of this book, in the end, knowing all this and being able to apply concrete strategies in order to have the best chances to maximize your profit.

CHAPTER 1: THE FUTURE OF FINANCE

Cryptocurrency, non-fungible token, blockchain, augmented reality... There are so many confusing terms out there that it is hard to know where to begin. Here, we will discuss everything you need to know about cryptocurrency, including how it came to be, and where it is headed in the future. You will learn in-depth about what it truly is, along with all its pros and cons.

Cryptocurrency

Cryptocurrency, in its simplest terms, is a digital manifestation of money. This concept can be difficult to grasp at first, especially considering we are so used to seeing physical copies of a bill or coin. In this case, there is no tangible leaflet or piece of metal.

So, doesn't this all seem a little bit fake? If you can't see it and you can't touch it, then how do you know it's even there? To answer this question, we must go back in time to consider what "money" even is.

A Brief History of Money

Before money was printed or coins were minted, humans used a bartering system to abandon and acquire goods. This, most historians agree, would be the most likely system in place around 3,000 years ago, although there is no definite proof of the system, making it effectively untraceable. The issue with this system was that trades were made difficult by the personal desires of the people involved: person #1 may want what person #2 has, however person #2 may not be willing to make the trade for the particular item that person #1 offers. This likely first brought humanity towards the idea of using some goods that seemed to have *universal value* for trades. The earliest examples of these *currencies* would be animal skins, weapons, and salts (Beattie, 2021).

Throughout the centuries, there was a shift towards the use of silver or gold as currency, since these items also had a rarity to them, and thus that same universal value as animal pelts once held. This idea of perceived value continues to be seen in history, as there was even a time during the 4th century B.C. when black pepper, dubbed the *King of Spices* was as valuable as gold and used as currencies, as it had just recently been discovered to Western Europe in the conquests of Alexander the Great. All this, just to say that money, in and of itself, has no true value other than what society places on it.

Taking this further, eventually humanity saw the shift between what has a *universal value* to what the *government* deemed to have value. Currencies became centralized to banks in this way and the physical copies of coins or, eventually, paper bills, were more receipts than anything, testifying that they were worth something. The true value was more of an idea than anything else.

However, there are still some problems, even with this monetary system. For one, it is fairly easy for criminals to trace and hack into a modern-day person's bank account and then send themselves as much money as they want. Physical copies of money also, when just passed around without the use of debit or credit, are, by nature, untraceable, and therefore shady deals profit much more from this.

Cryptocurrencies were first suggested in the 1980s, but the first digital coin appeared in 1995: Digicash, by David Chaum. It didn't flourish, similarly to subsequent attempts, such as Bitgold. These two first cryptocurrencies had one thing in common: they both were heavily encrypted for maximum protection between a money donor and recipient to make sure no illegal transactions were occurring. This was the early concept of *cryptography*, which is defined as the practice and study of encrypting information so that only those for whom it is intended can access it.

Bitcoin (BTC) was the first truly widespread cryptocurrency, developed in 2009 by an anonymous person or group with the pseudonym of Satoshi Nakamoto. With Nakamoto, the issue of the centralized system, which could be easily hacked and changed, was solved. The solution was thus created from the suggestion of a decentralized, peer-to-peer (P2P) network, using blockchain technology.

Starting out at a value of only 0.09 USD = 1 BTC, it reached an all-time high of 67 549.14 USD = 1 BTC in November 2021 (Edwards, 2021), although the market is still and will always be heavily uncertain with constant fluctuation.

The Inner-Workings of the Blockchain

Every single transaction on a cryptocurrency platform is stored as information on something called a *ledger*, which is a digital record. Each transaction on the ledger has a donor, a recipient, and the amount of money exchanged. The donor and recipient here are represented as highly encrypted codes.

Now, since the ledger is recording every single cryptocurrency transaction, this file quickly grows large in size. This is where the concept of *blockchain* comes into play. Blockchain is a way of storing the ledger into blocks, making the information quicker and easier for the computer to handle.

The cryptocurrency system's biggest advantage is its decentralization, accomplished by the P2P network. There is only one blockchain as there is only one record of all transactions by the specific currency, however there are hundreds of thousands of copies of this blockchain. The way the P2P network works is that people can "mine Bitcoin" or mine a different cryptocurrency by reserving a computer particularly to hold and update a copy of the blockchain. In exchange, they receive some cryptocurrency for it. This results in hundreds of thousands of computers, all individually updating the ledgers, and therefore there is not one *central* source of all transactions, rather making them transparent—although encrypted—to everyone. This system works so that if one copy of the ledger is different from the 99% of everyone else, then automatically foul play has been caught in the act and can be fixed, increasing the system's security.

Different Currencies

To get a better idea of how cryptocurrencies work, let's consider Canada and the Canadian dollar, or CAD. In contrast, across the world, Japan uses the Japanese yen, or JPY. They are both currencies by definition, but have different monetary values to these different countries. Similarly, cryptocurrencies are *money*, just as CAD or JPY, but represent different values, and in fact cryptocurrency is, more than anything, an umbrella term for thousands of different currencies.

Of these, the most well known, as well as the first successful one, is Bitcoin (BTC). It continues to be most widespread in its use, however it does compete for the top value. Altcoins are termed as cryptocurrencies that are modeled after Bitcoin, advertising slight changes to the system, such as a more specialized use, faster processing time, or better cryptography.

Ethereum (ETH), the most popular altcoin currency as of 2021, is on the rise and is the preferred platform for many NFTs and blockchain games. It boasts a more specialized use than Bitcoin, in that it is an entire platform (Ethereum) as well as a currency (Ether). This means that games can be built and used off the blockchain. These games or programs are called decentralized applications (dapps) and are the main draw of this type of currency. Ether is used to then maintain the dapps on the Ethereum platform, and can be traded like other cryptocurrencies.

Another altcoin commonly used is Litecoin (LTC). Litecoin uses "scrypt" proof of work to maintain their P2P decentralized network, which makes it easier to maintain on less powerful computers.

Finally, another couple of popular cryptocurrencies include, but are not limited to: Polkadot (DOT), Cardano (ADA), Bitcoin Cash (BCH), Binance Coin (BNB), Solana (SOL) and Ripple's XRP (XRP).

Pros and Cons of the Shift to Crypto

The biggest "pro" towards cryptocurrency is its decentralization coming from the P2P network. That the blockchain is regulated for and by the people allows not only a high level of security and difficulty for hacking and illegal transactions, but the transparency further allows the system to keep track of activity. In this way, crypto boasts being open and traceable through encrypted data, without losing its confidentiality. Moreover, unlike with physical money, transactions are able to be made anywhere in the world with virtually no limit on the amount, and these transactions can take less than half a day, therefore making it a convenient alternative to banks. Furthermore, transaction fees, interest rates, and exchange rates for cryptocurrency are all incredibly low, which is another advantage to the crypto shift above physical cash.

There are, however, some "cons" to the shift to cryptocurrency, which vary in severity from the sheer novelty of the system to serious issues that must be addressed. The first disadvantage of cryptocurrency is that it is incredibly energy-consuming. Because the P2P network is so large and involves so many computers running at high power all the time, vast amounts of electricity are being used to maintain it all, which is a highly concerning consequence to the environment.

Socially, cryptocurrencies are highly volatile and their prices can change drastically in the span of a single day. There have been cases of people investing their entire life savings into Bitcoin, just to lose it all. This is why an investor cannot depend on crypto-investments as a main income and should always be safe and responsible with their money as one cannot predict the future.

Cryptocurrency technology is constantly being improved and reworked. Faster technology, better algorithms, and different proofs of stake are being developed. These developers as well as crypto miners sometimes turn to be at odds with each other over issues, which can result in the split of a currency. Such was the case with Bitcoin, when it split, creating Bitcoin Cash (BCH), which believed in increasing the individual block sizes within the blockchain from 1MB to 8MB, in the hopes of increasing transaction speed. The issue is that when a cryptocurrency "forks" like this, the price of the two diverging currencies becomes uncertain and the investor must make the choice on whether they want to pull out and switch currencies, or if they want to choose which way to diverge with the tide. This will be touched more upon in Chapter 11.

How Cryptocurrency and the Blockchain Can Be Used

Not all companies accept cryptocurrency as a form of payment, however, as the years progress, more are willing to do so. Along with being able to simply buy goods, cryptocurrency can also be traded, either directly to a buyer or through a third party exchange broker. Coinbase and Kraken are examples of third party brokers, which will allow you to withdraw cash after the cryptocurrency has been deposited to them.

Specific to the Ethereum platform, because of the dapps and programs that can be built into it, there are also marketplaces that can be accessed through it and that exclusively trade using ETH. Most NFTs are sold on such marketplaces. Other dapp categories include: financial services to lend tokens for interest or borrow money, blockchain games, in which the user can play games and sell assets to earn ETH, and technology where users can earn ETH by browsing the Internet or renting out resources to expand the platform.

Where Are We Headed?

When adapting the Bitcoin mining system to the Ethereum platform, a problem was encountered where Ethereum desired a faster processing speed: around 1 block/15 seconds as opposed to Bitcoin's 1 block/10 minutes. The regular mining system, called *proof of work,* consumes too much electricity, and therefore a new system, called *proof of stake* was developed. The use of "validators" to check blocks in the blockchain could eventually make Ethereum a more environmentally-friendly cryptocurrency than Bitcoin in the long run.

A big fear and longstanding issue within the crypto community is the idea that the prized decentralization of the P2P system may be put in jeopardy. In the case of Ethereum in particular, most blockchain mining occurs by mass companies, who employ hundreds of employees to dedicate their time to it. Thus, the process has become more centralized, defeating the purpose of the system, and this remains an issue.

One of the biggest hurdles to overcome is acceptance by society. There is a lot of fear surrounding the use of cryptocurrency, as rumors spread about its use for criminal affairs, however this is mostly due to the spread of misinformation and lack of generally accessible knowledge on the industry. When explained incorrectly, the ideas of blockchain and digital money may seem overcomplicated, however, slowly, people are coming to terms that this is the future.

CHAPTER 2: WHAT IS THE METAVERSE?

The term "metaverse" has been trending around the Internet since Mark Zuckerberg's announcement of Facebook's rebranding to Meta. The apps of its subsidiaries, including some giants like Instagram, Whatsapp, and Oculus VR, now all display the Meta logo upon their startup. Other parts of the Internet are in an uproar by the cryptic and mechanical trailer in which Zuckerberg announced the metaverse. The ideas that surround it, though having been done before in certain respects to augmented and virtual reality, seem so unrealistic, verging on preposterous, that people cannot help but crack a joke. However, should he succeed along with other companies highly interested in the concept, the interest in the product is astronomical. Just like Bitcoin, which started off at a value of a mere 9 cents, early investments in the metaverse have the same potential to skyrocket in the long term.

A Brief History of Meta and the Metaverse

Meta

In 2004, Facebook was founded by Harvard University alumni Mark Zuckerberg, Eduardo Saverin, Dustin Moskovitz, Andrew McCollum, and Chris Hughes. It had an immediate effect: within one month, over half of the undergraduate students at their university were signed up for the platform. Not long afterwards, the app broadened its reach at the end of 2005, spreading all across the Western world, beyond just the U.S. The biggest insistence that Zuckerberg had, and probably one of the biggest reasons for the network's success, was the transparency of its users. This meant that it was forbidden to lie about identity or other aspects of one's life, and in this way, Facebook aimed to be a trustworthy way to know what a person was doing. Another big appeal of the service was that it was free to make a profile, but the primary source of revenue for Facebook is through advertisements, though this would cause privacy issues to be brought up in the future.

In 2008, Facebook surpassed MySpace as the most popular social media network on the Internet. Since then, it has grown to become a juggernaut on the Internet and society. On top of individual profiles, most companies also began setting up accounts to generate more traction for their businesses. Then, in 2012, Facebook became a public company, meaning that people could now buy stock in it. The company's value shot up by multi-billions of dollars following suit.

Instagram, another major social media platform more centered around pictures and short videos, was acquired by Facebook in April 2012 for $1B in cash and stock. Whatsapp was thereafter purchased by the company in February 2014 for $14B and Oculus was bought just a month later for $2B, Zuckerberg obviously seeing the potential as VR and social network opportunities.

On October 28th 2021, Mark Zuckerberg announced a major rebrand of his company, previously named Facebook, into Meta Platforms. This does not mean that any of the services under the company would change their own names, just the parent company. The first reason for this rebrand is the long-term plans for the metaverse project, in which full digital immersion is to be achieved. Nevertheless, there is also speculation that the rebrand has as a side goal to divert attention from all the past controversies now associated with the Facebook name, including the mining and sale of consumer information to interested companies in order to tailor advertisements, in hopes of being attached to a new venture of progress. These scandals had put Facebook in the spotlight as the poster child of bad technological practice and invasion of privacy through social media. Through the rebrand to Meta, news outlets and Internet critics believe the company is making another empty promise that they will change: A new name, a new brand, but the same old problematic actions are what they believe will come from this announcement.

However, in terms of the dream of the metaverse, Zuckerberg says in a press conference: "Over time, I hope that we are seen as a metaverse company and I want to anchor our work and our identity on what we're building towards," (Thomas, 2021).

The Metaverse

In 1992, just one year after the official beginning of the Internet, author Neal Stephenson released his science fiction book entitled "Snow Crash." This novel becomes the inspiration for Mark Zuckerberg's rebrand, as it describes a virtual reality world separate from real life, where the experience is still entirely life-like. These two worlds are interconnected in the novel, to the point where if something happens—say, a drug called "Snow Crash" was ingested—in the so-called "metaverse," it would also affect the actual person. Thus the idea for Zuckerberg's metaverse: a lifelike 3D immersion experience in which the user can do nearly anything in a virtual environment, whether it is work, games, or social gatherings.

Augmented and virtual reality (AR and VR) are not new ideas. There have been approaches to the metaverse concept through other games and platforms. Some of the most popular ones include: Minecraft, Fortnite, and Roblox. In these video games, a player can essentially do whatever they want, unrestricted to a certain extent by boundaries. This means that they are able to go wherever they want and carry out whatever actions they want as dictated by the limitations programmed into the game. These examples can also be multiplayer, meaning potential can expand tenfold by the addition of other players in the same world, where they can interact with each other just as they would in real-life, except it's not; it's virtual reality. In these games, players can simulate *life* itself without the worries of reality.

Meta already has some features that will be sustained in the metaverse. The 2014 acquisition of the company Oculus is one such example of a shift towards virtual reality, particularly with their main products: VR headsets. This hardware is placed over the user's eyes, transforming their entire field of vision into an interactive virtual landscape. Microsoft has also shown equal interest in the development of the metaverse. They have been developing extended reality projects (XR), which would include the use of holographic technology and avatars on their social and video conferencing service: Microsoft Teams. Other companies owned by Microsoft that approach the metaverse vision include Minecraft, Xbox, and Skype. The organization has also worked with the U.S. Army to develop VR headsets to aid in the training of soldiers.

In all these ways, humanity is not so far off from reaching the metaverse. The line between the physical and virtual is further blurred by the emergence of cryptocurrency, beginning in 2008 with the whitepaper for Bitcoin, and then 2009 with its official release. We already know all about cryptocurrency from the last chapter, however what we have not discussed is its impact towards the creation of the metaverse, although you can probably piece together a couple of ties already. First, the digitization of money places more dependency on the upkeep of the online realm—there is no need for banks or government-regulated transactions when paying crypto. In the metaverse, it is likely that this will also be the main type of currency accepted. In another case, the Ethereum platform is already quite similar to certain aspects of the metaverse. Dapps can be programmed directly onto the blockchain, making it a perfect marketplace for buying and selling art, digital assets, services, information, video game inventory, and more.

The metaverse is projected to be ready for testing and usage by the year 2035, which is not so far off as one may at first imagine, and this is because of all the ways in which the Internet is already approaching the concept as previously discussed. The process is also quickened because it will not just be Meta that is working on the project; Every single developer or company that builds AR or VR will be implicated and placed under the umbrella term of the "metaverse." This means that there will not be several metaverses, but rather everything that approaches the vision of Stephenson, Zuckerberg, and those like-minded will be by definition part of *the* metaverse.

In his Founding Letter for Meta, Zuckerberg (2021) says:

We've gone from desktop to web to mobile; from text to photos to video. But this isn't the end of the line. The next platform will be even more immersive [...]. We call this the metaverse, and it will touch every product we build. The defining quality of the metaverse will be a feeling of presence—like you are right there with another person or in another place. Feeling truly present with another person is the ultimate dream of social technology. That is why we are focused on building this.

The Impact of the Announcement

Zuckerberg's vision has been made clear to the people: He wants to aid in building a metaverse where people can have a complete virtual reality experience. The foreseen impacts on society, technology, finance and the environment will be discussed in Chapter 3, however there have already been ripples of change caused at the time of the announcement.

Society as a whole doubts if it is ready for such integration of technology into their everyday lives, and the subject can be controversial depending on the people involved in the discussion. First of all, those people who are already using metaverse-like technology such as interactive games or networks, are likely not so concerned about this shift. Those more unfamiliar with the workings of the Internet and those who fear that people will forget to live in reality are of concern. With the recent surge of children who become so addicted to their electronic devices and games that they cannot discern reality from fiction anymore, many parents and Senior citizens also doubt the value in such a tool, wondering if people will forget what makes them more than a machine.

Moreover, there are those who cannot forget Mark Zuckerberg's track record with his subsidiaries. Concerns about privacy and Internet safety are widespread as Facebook has been infamous for selling user data to companies in order to tailor advertisements. With the COVID-19 pandemic, Facebook had also seemed to be unconcerned with the spread of misinformation about safety, medically approved treatments, and the available vaccines on their platform.

In the eyes of other tech-savvy individuals, developers, and current avid users of virtual reality, the announcement of the metaverse was, more than anything, an attempt to steal credit from preexisting products as a last-minute effort to join the metaverse movement, which had thrived for the past decade before Zuckerberg's involvement. Current metaverse technology by smaller organizations were founded on the same concept of decentralization as cryptocurrencies, that is, there is no central power and thus are free from the centralized control that Meta's version may have. On the other hand, some people are quite excited at the traction that the announcement could bring to the movement, and the ways that the technology could improve with the amount of money that will be invested in it by such a large corporation.

By environmental standards, whether centralized or decentralized metaverse platforms boom in popularity, these systems require enormous amounts of electricity. At present, NFTs, mostly sold in the Ethereum blockchain, are under harsh criticism for the astronomical carbon emissions with which they are associated, because in order to receive a receipt for one art piece, huge amounts of cryptocurrency mining has to be completed on more than half a million potential different computers must be done to update the blockchain. The carbon footprint of these transactions, however, is debated, since different energy sources can be used to power the computers. It is estimated that around 70% of the energy is clean, thus decreasing environmental impact. However, to make this process sustainable in the long term, that other 30% must be addressed, and solutions must be designed.

Despite all the criticism, one thing is certain: Although the development and implementation of the metaverse is an ongoing project, and has been for the past couple decades by numerous individuals and small companies, the announcement of Facebook's involvement, as well as plans for other mega-companies to work on their own versions, has driven mass attention to the possible opportunities that it presents.

CHAPTER 3: THE ESTABLISHED METAVERSE

The metaverse strives to enhance daily life, interconnecting people more than ever before and revolutionizing the way people work, play, and socialize. Having this fairly new technology come into play can seem very daunting, however, we must wholeheartedly embrace—and even take advantage of—the future. The concept is further confusing as it still develops. In some ways, the metaverse has already begun with interactive games and cryptocurrency marketplaces, but in other ways like in the realms of VR and AR, which are not yet widespread in use, there is still a long way to go. The end goal, most can agree, is for the metaverse to take the place as a *better version* of the Internet. Taking a look at the projected impact of the metaverse's integration into daily life when it finally and fully establishes itself, we can make note of where we as a generation are headed.

Technological Impact

The metaverse presents itself on the pedestal of virtual and augmented reality technology. Many companies involved in building it, in terms of hardware, envision VR headsets, AR glasses, and similar technology in order to fully immerse the user in the experience. Instead of sitting in an online video call meeting, for instance, the user would be transported into a fully virtual, three-dimensional meeting room, where all participants, represented as avatars, can interact similarly to how they would if they were actually, truly in the same room together.

The gaming industry is one of the mediums that most fully understands the idea of the metaverse and has applied it several times through numerous platforms such as PC, console, mobile phone, or VR headset. In the future, there will likely be a shift towards a more widespread use of games for headsets, perhaps the world will also begin to see more specialized buildings pop up for VR rooms, which will be spaces for a player to motion around and play immersive games without the fear of breaking something or bumping into a real world object.

Metaverse technology, because of how immersive it needs to be in order to be viable to the consumer, must also adapt and improve drastically in the next few years upcoming to its release. Broadband speeds must become faster than ever, at more than 1GB/sec in order to produce a seamless experience (Vena, 2021). This may seem unattainable, but every day, technology gets more and more realistic, to the point where Disney can make movie scenes with avatars that are indistinguishable from real actors and that as soon as they are created, that software has already become outdated.

This brings on the next point: software. Microsoft, for example, has been developing Mesh on their Microsoft Teams app, which will add holograms of avatars to the platform. This is but a simple first step towards hologram integration into metaverse-focused applications.

Economical Impact

The economical impact of the metaverse can be divided in a couple different spaces. First, there is, of course, the boom in cryptocurrency usage that is expected, since this will be the main way in which goods will be distributed within the digital world. Another economical impact is the renovation of retail and online shopping platforms. Finally, there are also new products that will pop up and be able to be sold, whereas ten years ago, they would not be seen at all as valuables.

We've discussed cryptocurrency in depth, along with the stigma caused by myths of rampant crime due to its lack of central authority. The true nature of crypto consists of thriving digital marketplaces as is the case on Ethereum, to which the metaverse will act similarly, and perhaps even make more sense to people than current e-commerce. For example, NFTs are sold on Ethereum, and all that the buyer would receive is essentially a proof of partial ownership. Many people ridicule this sort of business because they do not understand its value, however, in the metaverse, this can come to make a bit more sense to these people. In a fully digital world, an NFT could be displayed in a virtual house, or the owner can charge crypto money for a viewing, similar to art shows or real art purchases in the real world.

Furthermore, retail and online shopping platforms can benefit from the metaverse revolution, as they can provide a better online experience, thus opening up their clientèle further than they would think imaginable. To better visualize this concept, a retail company's website could potentially use holographic and avatar technology to show the consumer what a clothing article would look like on their bodies, with size and height inclusion. The consumer would no longer be placing a gamble on the clothing when they put in an order, thus encouraging more purchases for the company. Having this type of virtual shopping environment is important since the COVID-19 pandemic, and improving this system would be greatly appreciated by the masses. Since 2020, in fact, many people were introduced to online shopping for perhaps the first time, and thus the market is ripe for improvement in order to stay with the times and stay afloat.

Finally, new products and new business opportunities will open up with the expansion of the metaverse. With this new virtual reality platform where people can represent themselves as avatars, there will be a cryptocurrency market for different outfits or looks that can be used for customization, similar to the clothing market of the real world. Other business ventures are sure to open up as well, particularly for coders and developers to create different apps or sites on the metaverse.

Social Impact

Similarly to the Internet, the metaverse is sure to be structured and maintained closely to how society molds it, and it is in the end the community which will be at the very heart of the technology. Through this new digital platform, solutions and innovations to common sectors will be made possible, interconnectivity between people will be stronger than ever, and there will be a wider acceptance of general technological progress despite being such a new concept and frightening to some, especially with science-fiction novels like *Snow Crash* or *Ready Player One* that depict tech-driven, dystopian worlds.

First off, through the metaverse, real-life sectors will become further accessible to the masses. We have already discussed how e-commerce will be revolutionized, but other areas will also see drastic improvement. In the education sector, for example, the user will be able to learn the theory of evolution from a virtual avatar of Charles Darwin, and be transported to the Galápagos Islands all from the comfort of one's own home. In another case, one could find themselves among the crowd during Martin Luther King Jr.'s famous "I Have a Dream" speech and learn about the civil rights movement in the United States. In addition to all this, the education sector will not be the only part of society that will change. In the healthcare department, for example, the use of AR and VR could potentially enhance the proficiencies of medical tools and procedures. These tactics are also starting to be used for the training of first responders. There are many more ways in which metaverse technology could improve humanity, and many solutions that have yet to be developed.

The next possibility for the future of the metaverse in terms of social change is a heightened connectivity between people. With the invention of the Internet and social media, people can talk or write to each other from across the world in a matter of seconds. However, with the metaverse, users will be able to virtually interact with each other much more fluidly in a three-dimensional space where their experience will be as though they are in the same room. This idea is similar to what certain metaverse-like games are doing right now—like Minecraft or Roblox—showing the world that this technology and this future is not so far off as it may at first seem. In fact, Meta has made this new way of presenting social media its main focus ever since its name change from Facebook.

As the years progress, a societal consensus of the good that the metaverse can and will provide to humanity should develop. With enough resources like books, articles, and videos explaining what the metaverse is, people will eventually abandon the fear of becoming slaves to technology and accept it as a part of their everyday lives, designed to make them easier, more convenient. This will also discredit misinformation about the current technology that has already been established, as well as clearing up information about cryptocurrencies that will be the main source of currency of the future.

Finally, the metaverse itself will become heavily creator-oriented in the long term, since this project will connect the entire world and will, thanks to experienced developers and small companies, maintain a decentralized system for the people, by the people. There is controversy that may come to surround this, with tension developing between creators and investors. As can be seen in the modern-day NFT world, some artists are not happy that their work can be bought as tokens and then resold. However, in general, just like how anyone can create a website, video, or game and post it online, so it will be with the metaverse, likely with direct blockchain coding so that these games can be connected to cryptocurrencies. In this way, creators will be the lifeblood of the metaverse.

Environmental Impact

Environmental consequences are inevitable to most actions and innovations. In the case of the metaverse, there is some good impact, such as reduced need for travel, more green energy jobs, and the avoidance of dangerous situations with virtual training. On the other hand, the same problems that can be seen with electricity needs of blockchain mining and data processing will come up with the metaverse as environmental detriments. All things considered, there is also the possibility that future efforts to save the environment, as well as technological innovation and improvement with sustainability in mind, would be able to change the course that we are on and allow society the best of both the real world and the virtual one.

So, how can the metaverse help the environment? First of all, the more people that work and hold meetings in an interactive virtual platform, there will be less of a need to go into a physical workplace. For the typical 9 to 5 office job, most work will be able to be shifted online, which will allow the employee to do their job from the comfort of their own home. There is also the possibility that complete metaverse-integrated jobs will appear, having to do with maintenance of the crypto marketplace and possibly even sustainability-centered technological research positions. Moreover, dangerous and unsustainable workplace training will be able to be done virtually, which will save the environmental impact of actual on-the-job activity that will no longer be fully necessary.

Nevertheless, there are some environmental concerns associated with the development of the metaverse and its maintenance. It has been mentioned before that blockchain mining and NFT transactions in particular require huge amounts of electricity, which can increase global carbon emissions. In the case of the metaverse, the same concepts apply: this is a high-power system, and therefore requires a very high processing speed. Researchers at the University of Massachusetts have found that common AI models of the modern day emit up to 626,000 lbs. of carbon dioxide to be trained (GlobalData Thematic Research, 2021). Experts at Lancaster University say that, if the video game industry shifts to a metaverse-like platform on the cloud as technology currently is, by 2030, there will be a 30% increase in carbon emissions caused by gaming.

In the end, there is still hope. Nobody can predict the course of technology or sustainability advancements, but in order to solve a problem, society must first be made aware of it. This is why it is important to know the facts and work collectively to find solutions, as the metaverse represents incredible social, economical, and technological progress, but it would not be possible without being able to find a balance with the real world and its real environment that is the lifeblood of us all.

CHAPTER 4: HOW AUGMENTED REALITY WILL WORK IN THE METAVERSE

One has surely heard of the *Pokémon Go* craze of 2016, catching Pokémon, monster-like creatures, that have been transposed through phone cameras onto real-world surfaces. Or maybe they have used the *Google Lens* feature on their Android mobile phone to identify the name of a certain plant, insect or animal that they found in the woods behind their house. These are just some popular examples of how augmented reality, or AR, has begun to integrate itself in our reality for the past decade. At its core, the idea of AR is to take the real world and transpose virtual elements overtop of it to, say, augment or enhance it.

In the metaverse, the concept of AR will be even more widely utilized than it is today. In fact, games like *Pokémon Go* and apps like *Google Lens* would fit in nicely as metaverse technology. In this chapter, the inner-workings of augmented reality will be explained in depth, as well as the steps that will be taken in the future to achieve the full AR potential, and how AR can come to benefit the metaverse and humanity along with its timeline.

How Does Augmented Reality Work?

Augmented reality consists of both hardware and software. The hardware of AR usually ranges from just a regular phone, PC, or tablet, to actual specialized devices designed for specific software. The user can usually point whatever device they are holding towards a surface, and it will detect whatever is there through computer vision technology so that images superimposed on it will be placed correctly.

A good modern-day example are filters on social media platforms like Snapchat or Instagram. All a person has to do is point the camera towards their face and then, through camera technology, their features, like the nose, eyes, mouth, and eyebrows, are all recognized. The app can then superimpose AR through the camera lens, like growing the eyes, placing dog ears on top of the head, causing an animation to trigger when the mouth opens, etc.

Hardware

The hardware necessary for AR consists of a camera of sorts, through which the real-world image and virtual elements can be seen as a live camera feed. Other than the camera, some other useful components are GPS (Global Positioning System), microphone, processor, and display. Over the years, there have been other specialized systems created for AR. One of the most exciting ones is the SixthSense technology, announced in 2009 by MIT Media Lab's Fluid Interfaces Group. It was a rough prototype consisting of everyday products: a mirror, smartphone, small projector, and a camera.

The projector emits an image, and by holding up fingers with colored thumb caps–worn by the user–up to the camera, the components of the image could be moved simply by the movement of the hands and fingers. Any surface onto which the projector could project would have the potential to become interactable. The SixthSense technology represents just one way in which hardware could become specialized in the future to accommodate peak AR experiences.

Another example of a perhaps more refined and complete project is that of Microsoft Hololens, which is an actual headset designed with sensors and optics to detect real-life objects and allows a person to interact with holograms in front of them.

Software

Software is perhaps the most important part of producing an AR product, and realistically, it is unlikely for a majority of the population to buy specialized hardware as soon as the metaverse releases, since it will be relatively new to many. Therefore, AR had to find a way to adapt to what people already nearly all have: Smartphones. Snapchat, Instagram, Pokémon Go, and Google Lens are software apps adapted for phones that have shown immense popularity among the masses.

We have already established that augmented reality works by computer vision. The camera live feed is rendered by the device, determining 3D position, depth of view, and orientation of objects in focus. Registration tools, such as motion sensors, define where virtual images can be superimposed. Machine-learning algorithms learn where certain things are placed within the real world and will track them as they move around in the camera view. All these elements come together on the output device, which displays the final AR feed.

Different Types of AR

There are a couple different ways that augmented reality can work. The first is something called "marker-based AR." This consists of a custom app that is specially designed to recognize a certain object, or "marker." Examples include QR codes or logo recognition.

There is also the exact opposite of marker-based AR, namely markerless AR. There are no markers here, and so the camera does not detect a specific thing. Instead, a virtual 3D object can be projected into a rendered space. Examples of how this method of AR can be used include arrangement of virtual furniture to visualize a furnished space in an empty room, or orientation of a digital hologram in the palm of your hand.

The last type of common AR technology is called "projector-based AR." This acts in the way that the SixthSense prototype was discussed earlier, where the AR relies much more on the real world, projecting hologram-like images on objects. Practically, this type of augmented reality is used in light guide systems.

The Developer's Standpoint

So how do people and companies code AR technology? First, in marker-based AR, coding is relatively inexpensive and easy to do in comparison to other types. This is because the camera is searching for a specific object that is often distinct from the rest of its environment.

In markerless AR, a lot more power is dispensed by the device. There is also slow rendering time, since there is a lot more to do by the phone than in marker-based AR. It also depends on flat, textured surfaces (Schechter, 2020).

Finally, in projector-based AR, the process becomes more complicated. This process uses projection mapping, in which the projection has to create a digital overlay across surfaces. It also requires a knowledge beyond just camera devices and camera vision tech, but also knowledge of projector hardware.

How Will We Achieve Full AR?

In many ways, the foundation for an AR world has already been laid out. There is a lot of technology that has been developed that already works fairly well in the modern day. However, there are still improvements to be made, and these will further be possible with the boom of the metaverse and all the attention it will get from consumers and developers alike.

The first thing to note is that coding and creating augmented reality programs is not a simple process. Computer vision technology actually comprises a whole area of tech innovation and study. While it is simple for humans to look through a camera lens and identify what is in the feed, computers have a hard time doing so, and therefore finding ways of getting computers to read this data and render it is a hot topic that is being thoroughly researched, but the progress has been enormous thus far. Achieving full AR will have much to do with perfecting this technology and syncing it with camera and real-world movement. By playing with AR games like *Pokémon Go*, for example, there will no longer be any glitching or vibrating of the holograms caused by the sensitivity of the motion sensors.

Moreover, achieving full AR looks like complete integration into social media. One of Mark Zuckerberg's biggest goals for the transformation of Facebook through the lens of the metaverse is by the creation of avatars, superimposed over real people, where users can change and enhance how they look with digital additions however they want. For example, if a person wanted a giraffe head, they could add this head through AR technology and walk around, and then people who also use Facebook could see the virtual avatar through their camera.

Social media is not the only place where augmented reality can infiltrate and fully transform the industry. The use of AR in sectors such as healthcare, offices, and education have already all been discussed in Chapter 3. Complete AR integration is another example of how the technology could reach its full potential in the future, when the technology is further improved, as it can aid in finding new solutions and new tactics to age-old problems, like teaching the next generations or training new workers effectively. In fact, in terms of education and teaching new generations, the idea of enhanced visual learning has some science behind it. It is estimated that around 80% to 90% of a person's knowledge comes from their vision (Porter and Heppelmann, 2017b).

The Benefits of an AR World

The AR world will benefit humanity heavily, which is why the metaverse leans so heavily on its concepts, along with the technology behind VR, or virtual reality. The benefits to the healthcare, education, and military sectors from AR in the real world along with its specific applications here will also be discussed.

Healthcare

In the healthcare sector, products using AR technology can be used to visualize internal features and train new employees. In terms of visualizing internal features, there is the example of AccuVein technology. AccuVein senses heat patterns in a patient's veins and superimposes the patterns on top of the patient, thus allowing the medical official to find an area of interest in the circulatory system. Since the use of this kind of technology, successful needle sticks on the first try have increased by 45% (Porter and Heppelmann, 2017b). This also reduces the amount of "escalations," which is when the situation worsens by an improper needle stick. In terms of training new employees, augmented reality has the potential to train workers step-by-step on how to complete certain tasks, allowing more time for full-time employees to work elsewhere instead of providing constant assistance to trainees.

Education

The benefits that the education system could receive from AR culminate to one main conclusion: Visual representation of educational concepts will increase retention for many people for whom this is their main way of learning. The science behind it is due to each human's individual cognitive load, which refers to their capacity to complete mental tasks. The learning process, once information attempts to enter into the cognitive load, first goes through a cognitive distance, which is the time between when the information is presented to when the brain processes and understands it. In comparison to audible or written information, visualization has been found to be the way to the shortest cognitive distance for most people, which is why AR is so promising to education systems.

Additionally, AR has the added feature of interactivity. Being able to interact with knobs, buttons, etc. are great tools for kinesthetic learners, thus even further expanding the scope of the technology to teaching new generations.

Military

Military training and its utilization of AR had been briefly touched upon in Chapter 2. First of all, in-person training is usually expensive, requires a collective time scheduling for both mentor and trainee, and the information is not always absorbed on the first try by the student. The military uses AR as a safe way to simulate warfare for training purposes, and have actually been one of the first and most receptive adopters of this type of technology. Examples of hardware utilized include helmet mounted displays and smart glasses (Bonson and Chandler, n.d.).

Head-mounted augmented reality displays also go beyond simple training in the military. For example, these AR could be used for reconnaissance of a terrain to construct virtual blueprints or satellite views that the soldier can follow to avoid as much danger as possible.

CHAPTER 5: RISKS AND CHALLENGES

As it is with any new, big ideas, there are bound to be issues that arise, whether direct or indirect. In the case of the rise of the metaverse and wanting to be a part of it all, there are also some risks and challenges of which to be made aware. Some of these risks are quite similar to issues that we can already see with the Internet and social media, and others are completely new. As for challenges, developers will face many difficulties in building the technology that this innovative platform requires in order to seamlessly integrate itself into the lives of the masses, just as the Internet had done a couple decades ago.

Social Risk

Addiction

With all the advancements of the digital world, people—and, in particular, youth—find themselves drawn to technology. Therapists now deal with thousands of children who are, at various levels, so indoctrinated to their devices that, to varying degrees, they cannot live in the real world normally. With the rise of the Internet and all the good it brought with it, also came new problems, and one such is that of addiction. Whether Internet Addiction Disorder (IAD) qualifies as a true mental illness, however, remains a hot debate.

In 2016, Common Sense Media, a nonprofit organization designed to provide reviews of technology and movies for families, discovered from a survey that around 50% of teenage participants felt "addicted" to their phones, and that 75%of these people felt the urge to immediately reply to notifications (Robb, 2016). However, most of these individuals would not be using the word "addiction" in the same way as substance abuse may make a person chemically addicted by altering the brain. True addiction would be to push out everything else from that person's life, not being able to function normally socially or physically, and need an increasing amount of the substance as time progressed. This is much rarer when it comes to the Internet, which is why it is often not classified as causing "addiction."

This being said, there are children who are deeply affected by the amount of screen-time they receive. Some children arrive in therapy clinics because they truly can no longer tell the difference between what is real and what is virtual.

However, even this is debated as whether or not the effects were truly caused by access to the online realm, since these children may also have other underlying issues or disorders that have passed unchecked, and this in combination with screen-time has brought to light new symptoms. Either way, the best way to understand a child who the parent feels spends too much time on technology is to consult professionals in psychology and child therapy.

So, why are online games, media, and apps so addicting? Well, this is by design; the more time users spend on a platform, the more money that platform can potentially make either from advertisements, in-app purchases, or by other methods. Video game companies often specifically create "compulsory loops" that make the player want to continue playing on and on. Expectation, leading to reward, releases dopamine in the brain and makes the user feel good, which also leads to them wanting to continue using the technology (Smith, n.d.). Examples of rewards could be completing a level of a video game or getting "likes" on a social media post as a sort of validation. The inconsistency and dependency on the user to achieve these rewards also makes the experience more exciting, thus increasing dopamine.

The metaverse plans to make technology more interactive and more lifelike than ever. It will also not only boost social media activity but will encourage people to spend even longer periods of time on its platforms than even the modern Internet. There is thus the high risk of increasing dependency on technology, especially by the youth, whose minds are still moldable and underdeveloped. This posts the social risk of new generations that will not be able to function outside of the virtual world as easily as the generations that did not have virtual and augmented reality integrated into their early lives.

The issue becomes even more nuanced in debate: Is this truly a problem with the industry, that purposely makes their technology addicting in order to keep user retention? Or rather, is this risk, instead of placing the blame on the metaverse or the Internet itself, a responsibility of parental management? After all, it is the parents who decide how much screen-time a child receives, and it is the parents who buy the devices. In this way, it can be debated that parents should be responsible for how their child interacts with technology.

Social Media

When looking out at the future of the metaverse, the social media world only seems to improve, becoming more interactive and easily accessible than ever. As mentioned, however, addiction may also become more rampant. Additionally, there is a significant challenge in successfully transferring an already large and established user database to a whole new platform. Finally, many of the problems that modern social media faces, such as concerns of privacy or safety, will not simply disappear by, say, innovating the technology that it uses or changing the name of the company.

First of all, the addiction to social media has already been touched upon; that idea of "likes" on a post releasing dopamine to the account owner. However, unlike some iPad games or browsing movies and videos, social media does have a very strong connecting aspect, bringing together people from around the world who would have never met otherwise, and allowing them to talk, exchange ideas, and learn from each other. In this case, the main issue is not something so easily overcome. The idea of FOMO, that is, *fear of missing out*, has been amplified, since people feel they *have* to keep up with all the memories of their friends, for fear of being left in the dark to something interesting. In the metaverse, where there will be so much more to see, FOMO sentiments will definitely only increase.

The challenge of transporting an established user base to another platform will be further explained in the *Developers' Challenges* part of this section, however it remains a social risk that the metaverse will inevitably undertake. In the most relevant current case, Meta is already seeing issues in its rebrand. Their main website, Facebook, still remains the face of the company, and therefore, as it stands, nobody really associates Mark Zuckerberg with the word "Meta" at all, except maybe in a mocking sense. Something similar happened in the past with another big company, Google, which, in 2015 renamed its parent company to Alphabet, Inc. in order to expand further than being a search engine. Just like with Meta, though, to the general public, the company is referred to as Google since most consumers don't care about the bureaucracy of the organization.

Finally, problems that social media presently face may be amplified with the dawn of the metaverse. Facebook was under fire when it announced its rebrand to Meta, since many critics speculated this change was in large part due to the infamy associated with the current name. Facebook had become notorious for selling the personal information of their users to large corporations in order to send them tailored, personalized ads. This was all done with the false promise that consumers would be able to have control over how their information was shared by sifting through settings. So, the world went crazy when Facebook rebranded, and it seemed like just that: changing the name so as to dissociate from bad press without actually making any underlying changes. How can one thus expect companies to act any differently—especially when it pays so handsomely—when the metaverse will just require even more personal information from users, as it truly becomes a virtual self.

This is not the only issue with social media that will be transferred to the metaverse. Internet safety has been a widespread concern since it first came online. That people can pretend to be whomever they want is a frightening thought: anyone with whom you have an online conversation could be completely different in real life to how they present themselves therein. With Facebook, measures have been taken to try and avoid this at all costs, since it undermines the very principles on which it was founded, by vetting all accounts to make sure that they are run by real people providing their real information, which is, as has just been discussed, a whole different issue in itself, but works to keep out bot-run profiles. Other metaverse platforms cannot be expected to take the exact same measures as one company, and so this begs the question: if you get attached to a life-like holographic persona in the virtual realm, and you discover that it is all falsified with malicious intent, then this would be even more damaging and harder to discover than it would be on the current Internet.

Environmental Risk

The environmental risk of the metaverse lies in blockchain mining, and one of the main concerns of developers should be to find a way to completely base the process on clean, reusable, sustainable energy if they have hopes of bringing their wide-scope dream to life.

The Developers' Challenges

Coding and Engineering

There have already been significant advancements not only in sandbox-like environments as is the case with games like Minecraft or Roblox, but also in AR and in cryptocurrency dapps—platforms like Ethereum allow direct coding straight onto the blockchain. However, this practice of blockchain coding is not so widespread or well-known as of late. That blockchain coding is quite difficult and that developers must confront their personal morality on the unsustainable qualities of their work are all risks that the metaverse must overcome in order to grow.

Growing to Be the Next Internet

In order to grow to be the next bigger and better Internet, which is the end goal of all this metaverse talk, there are many challenges along the way. The biggest one may be that of transferring established user bases to a whole new, different platform, in particular consideration of the demographic of those databases. Other difficulties include: keeping the platform decentralized, creating interoperability, and monetary issues.

Facebook remains the most popular social media platform as of 2021, however fewer youth under 18 are signing up. The demographic from 19 to around 25 years of age is the largest, and this tapers down as age increases, but it was found that many people of middle-age or older create accounts every day. Since Facebook has turned into a more adult-minded platform in general, there is some risk involved in sudden change, especially considering that VR demographics—those for whom the metaverse truly excites—are mostly young adults (Digital in the Round, 2021). These Facebook users already feel at home with the current face and it is difficult to imagine them so readily accepting a complete change in the norm.

Another difficulty that developers of the metaverse face is that age-old struggle of digital communities in keeping the system decentralized. With so many companies seeing the value and the monetary opportunity in control of the metaverse, in order to maintain balance, there must be no single power or authority of the virtual playground.

With the concept of decentralization also arises interoperability, a necessary advancement in technology that must be made in order to establish the fundamentals of a viable metaverse. Interoperability relates to a user being able to move from one app to another with the same avatar and profile. This has to be a collective effort from developers of all metaverse projects, since they all have to together find a way to let a user travel between their platforms whilst retaining their same profile.

Finally, the metaverse is *expensive*. If some virtual worlds want to be realistic in order to be more attractive to the first-time consumer, the cost of digital assets is high. This is perhaps why the involvement of such a big company as Meta is exciting for some of those pursuing the metaverse: it is a big source of funds. Still, monetary challenges also remain as a boundary for hopeful developers who would otherwise love to try their hand at coding for the platform of the future. There is so much work to get the idea of lifelike social avatars to interact in a way that is not so completely artificial as well. On platforms that already exist like *Second Life*, player avatars do not provide the same freedom of movement as a real person simply because all actions must be coded and animated. To further and further approach life-likeness, coding and animating budgets are bound to become more expensive as well.

CHAPTER 6: MAIN AND UPCOMING PROJECTS

We are approaching the conclusion of all the general information surrounding the metaverse, Meta, and cryptocurrency projects. To end off and leave you with everything there is to know about where tech is headed, we will discuss the major apps that are leading the industry towards the metaverse. These include social platforms and video games.

Minecraft, Roblox, and Fortnite

Minecraft, Roblox, and Fortnite are three incredibly popular games with youth as of the past decade, each easily fitting as some of the most played games of 2021, with Minecraft being the most sold game of all time, at around 234 million sales (GamingSection, 2020).

The appeal of these three games, and more so with Minecraft and Roblox, is that there is no true goal or purpose. Though there is a huge market for RPGs and story-based games, in Minecraft and Roblox, people keep coming back because what truly makes the game is the playerbase's involvement. In Minecraft, a player can either play in a "Survival" mode, singleplayer or multiplayer, where they essentially act as the hero of an untouched and unique, randomly-generated world. In this world, they must gather resources to survive, and although there is technically an end boss fight, players can do, build, and act however they want, which is why they will usually keep playing on that world even after completing all the main "goals" that the game has set in place. In the other game mode that Minecraft offers, "Creative" mode, the player is granted infinite resources and basically "plays God" in the world, being able to build or destroy anything and fly anywhere in the world. There is no point to this game mode other than letting creativity and imagination guide whatever the player chooses to do.

There is even more to do in both Minecraft and Roblox due to community involvement. People invested in the game can make public servers, with their own sets of rules, guidelines, stories, or minigames that are ready to be accessed and played by the masses. These servers can even profit off of its player base by offering optionable, purchasable perks. This concept, one may realize, quite closely approaches the ideal of the metaverse at a smaller scope: one centralized account is able to access hundreds of decentralized, differently-led worlds that are completely crowd-created and crowd-funded.

Fortnite's metaverse looks a little bit different from these other two games. It is mostly a battle royale type of game, where players are dropped into a world that acts as an arena, and then must compete to be the last one standing. This is its main gaming element. However, Tim Sweeney, the CEO of Epic Games that created Fortnite, says that Fortnite is a metaverse game because it also incorporates non-gaming events (Bradley, 2021). For example, the game hosts a number of in-game events, such as concerts that actual artists have put on, that were attended by millions of players watching through the eyes of avatars on the virtual platform.

Sandbox

Sandbox is a leader in Ethereum blockchain-linked games, being a world-building, *sandbox* virtual playground centered around building and creating art. It originated as a mobile game for phones and tablets before expanding to the PC platform as well. It uses SAND currency, specific to its universe. People can buy plots of land on the game where they can either create virtual minigames or art galleries to sell NFTs or charge for viewing. In this way, they are heavily linked to the NFT marketplace, and thus artists and designers profit from this platform. There are also "Alpha passes" which are dropped to only 5,000 people, where they get the opportunity to compete in games in order to win SAND tokens (Ferrari, 2021).

The game is also looking to become fully decentralized and crowd-controlled in the next few years, and the developers would like to see it completely develop its own economy with SAND. Already, the user base as of 2021 comprises over 16,000 players and The Sandbox has partnered with dozens of different big companies, who all buy plots of land to further advertise their real-life businesses and wares.

Second Life

Second Life, developed in 2003, is arguably the first metaverse-like world to pop up online. As of 2021, there are almost 1 million players in its digital world, which, like the other platforms mentioned, is an open-world sandbox-type game. It does not have a specific goal, as the user will have to figure out how they want to use it for themselves. The difference is: this game is not about building. It is much more focussed on social interactions and connections than the previous apps mentioned thus far. Second Life boasts being used by many current companies as a place for meetings and business discussions. In more informal circumstances, there are many communities established in the world, such as music clubs, roleplaying groups, and virtual cinemas to name a few.

The way in which Second Life makes money is through an online marketplace, where users can buy and sell outfits, pets, home decor, and more.

Second Life as a game also gives a good view into some of the risks and challenges that the metaverse may face by sheer similarity to the concept. There have been issues related to the social aspect and anonymity of the game in that it is difficult to both moderate and keep the power decentralized in the hands of the community. There have been virtual riots and sexual content that had not been completely banned, making it very much an adult platform, and it highlights an issue that had been lightly touched upon in Chapter 5: if an entire community is given the power to do whatever they want online, then someone is bound to abuse it.

VRChat

VRChat is a virtual social platform that has been on the rise in the VR headset gaming community. It allows the user, who wears a headset, to explore and create worlds, create avatars, make friends and join communities all from a singular platform. From people who play on this app for hundreds of hours, there have been some pretty interesting notes on VR, which may go against what someone who had never or have rarely used it may think. One such discovery was that, though what a user may think is the future of virtual reality are hyper-realistic graphics and incredible, beautiful worlds and avatars, this is actually very taxing on the brain. Regular users of VR seem to naturally gravitate towards simpler graphics simply because there is less information to process at once. VRChat definitely shows that there is a place for all sorts of art and assets on the metaverse.

Decentraland

Decentraland boasts itself as being a—and perhaps the first—fully decentralized open-world game that is completely run by its users. Like The Sandbox, it runs on the Ethereum blockchain but uses its own currency, called MANA, for its marketplace. MANA acts as a governing token: whenever changes or updates must be made to the software, a voting system occurs with all those that possess MANA. Examples of votes that are held include policy changes, auctions for land, and development subsidies, all for in-world effects. The use of governing tokens acts to keep the fate of the game in the hands of the users so that the developers do not become a centralized power to the game.

There is another currency type used in Decentraland other than MANA, and they are actually the trade of special NFTs called LAND, which work as plots of virtual land. A main function of the game itself is to take empty plots of LAND, renovate them and build stuff on them, and then sell them. Other players can visit different plots, socialize with each other through messaging, voice chat, and gesturing. In general, the game functions as an investment opportunity hub, where people can also buy LAND and become its landlord; say, if someone wants to build a shop because of the in-game location and coordinates of that area, then they'd have to pay a rent to the owner of the LAND. This is yet another way to make money off these in-game NFTs. In general, buying LAND has become quite expensive due to its success, with the cheapest plot as of December 2021 going for $4,000 and this also because there are a limited amount of plots available to buy in the world.

Decentraland is the second most popular game built on the Ethereum blockchain, and stands in the Top 3 with The Sandbox and Axie Infinity.

Axie Infinity

Axie Infinity is the most popular blockchain game as of 2021 and continues to grow. Unlike The Sandbox or Decentraland, which are games based on the investment in NFTs and visual assets, Axie Infinity is a battle game. The idea is that players can collect NFTs of little monster characters, which then compete against other players' monsters, or "Axies." However, in comparison to The Sandbox or other games, it has become quite expensive to play due to its success: one needs at least three axies to play, each costing hundreds of dollars. Other than Axies, people can also buy land and items.

Axies can be bred and sold on the marketplace along with love potions that can be farmed, necessary for the breeding process. However, other than with marketplace transactions, there are ways in which players can make money. Battling in tournaments against other axies, for example, has prizes up for stake.

The biggest market, representing 40% of the player base, of Axie Infinity comes from the Philippines. For these people, particularly when the COVID-19 pandemic hit, being able to shift to online work on the decentralized player-paid and player-created game instead of having to go overseas has been a lifesaver.

Star Atlas

Star Atlas is different from the other blockchain games listed because it is not actually programmed into Ethereum. Rather, it runs on a different cryptocurrency chain, called Solana (SOL), which is much faster at processing transactions and comes at a much cheaper price in comparison to Ethereum. For this reason, Solana as a cryptocurrency has every chance to become just as popular or even overtake Ethereum, as it is relatively new, being officially launched only in March of 2020.

The game is an NFT-based science-fiction metaverse experience where players join a faction and try to outsmart the other players. Players gather resources, solve challenges, and go on journeys. Through the creation of groups or small factions with other people, there can be the formation of decentralized autonomous organizations (DAOs), where they can govern their own regions, on which they would build cities or create micro-economies. All assets acquired in-game can also be resold by the players, giving them complete ownership. This, beyond the goal of decentralization and having a completely player-run system, also gives a monetary incentive for participation.

Another way in which Star Atlas differs from some other blockchain games is that it runs on dual currency: ATLAS and POLIS. ATLAS tokens are the in-game economy, allowing the purchase of assets and NFTs. On the other hand, POLIS tokens are used for governance, meaning that people who hold POLIS will be able to vote on decisions related to updates and development. This is one of the ways in which Star Atlas encourages decentralization, by giving its user base the power to influence its future.

Meta: Facebook, Instagram, Whatsapp, and More

We all know that Facebook has been rebranded to Meta Platforms now. This means that, in the future, all the social media companies under its acquisition will be shifting into a metaverse-like vision. For Facebook, this means avatars interacting with each other in a virtual space. However, for other platforms like Instagram or Whatsapp, who are also child companies of Meta, how will things change?

Well, it is not completely clear. Although Mark Zuckerberg has said that Meta will be a metaverse-centered company, there is a large user base on both Instagram and Whatsapp who may not be so accommodating of changes. For one, Instagram is completely based on sharing pictures, and so there is not much benefit to switching to a more virtual or interactive experience. Whatsapp also does not quite fit into the image of the metaverse, as it is primarily just a messaging app, of which the appeal is that people from across the world and across different phone brands can text each other without worrying about extra fees. With the announcement still fresh in people's minds from October 2021, there are still many unknowns that have yet to come to light. One thing is certain: Meta's Facebook being such a huge cultural phenomenon and the company itself investing so much of itself into the metaverse means that big change is bound to occur in the years to come.

What Does This Teach Us?

In general, some aspects of all the games and apps mentioned have some similarities, refining the image that people have about the metaverse. First, they all fit into the category of "sandbox" games, where rules about where to go and what to do are dependent on whatever the player themselves decides. Another similarity in the games is that they all have their own separate marketplaces that are apart from the game but allow it to generate its own economy. In the case of blockchain games, these elements are integral to the experience, however in games that are simply proto-metaverse, like Second Life or Minecraft, the purchases are just perks to make the experience more enjoyable and are not for everyone. NFTs also have taken on their own life, further than just the online art market of Ethereum, to prove their usefulness in various games, which may make them easier to comprehend to a wider variety of people.

CHAPTER 7: THE BASICS OF INVESTING IN CRYPTO

With all the relevant knowledge of the current and predicted states of cryptocurrency and technological advancements of the Internet, including information on the metaverse's progress timeline and current projects that already fit in with it, it is finally time to start on the real question: how can you make money from it all? In this section of the book, we will be looking over how to find areas in which to invest, how much money should you spend, how to divide investments, and how to place your first investments.

How to Acquire Your First Crypto

Foremost, there are tons of different areas to invest in cryptocurrency. As discussed in Chapter 1, there are thousands of different cryptocurrencies, each with their own advantages and disadvantages. Bitcoin is of course the first and most popular choice, however 1 BTC is worth tens of thousands of dollars in most physical currencies, which makes it difficult to get into the market without doing mining in order to earn some by work, or already being in a financial position where you can spend a lot of money on such a volatile market as cryptocurrency. However, it is widely accepted in many markets and remains to be worth a lot of money. All-time highs are still also regularly being beaten.

Ethereum is the next popular choice, as the second biggest cryptocurrency market of 2021. Rather than relying on the peer-to-peer system of Bitcoin, it is the main platform on which dapps can be programmed directly onto the blockchain, expanding the market and the possibilities ever further. Through the acquisition of an Ethereum wallet, the world of NFTs and most of the biggest, already-established, blockchain games are both opened up, and with them, more opportunities for investment.

Other cryptocurrencies, such as Solana, also act as platforms on which apps can be directly programmed into the blockchain. In Solana's case, it is a newer currency, boasting faster transaction speeds and cheaper costs.

Do I Have to Buy Cryptocurrency?

Let's face it: Cryptocurrencies are expensive, especially the successful ones. However, as the saying goes: "The best time to start was yesterday. The next best time is now." (Unknown).

The purchase of cryptocurrency from a cryptocurrency exchange or payment service is the easiest and fastest way to begin your investment journey, but is not the only option and does not come without its own difficulties, and is therefore not suited to everyone. For networks like Bitcoin or Ethereum, you're getting into the thousands of dollars for a single coin. For other networks like

Dogecoin, the exchange rate is usually fairly cheap, however, it is an incredibly volatile market and the coin itself has never surpassed even the value of $1 USD as of 2021. Still, this means that, if one were to buy a large amount of Dogecoin for a couple cents, and decided to cash out when it increased, say, tenfold for a couple dozen cents, then you still receive ten times the amount of cash you invested. The opposite is also true, if it is bought at a couple dozen cents and keeps going down tenfold, then you may lose all but one tenth of the money you invested. This logic is true for all currencies.

A couple trusted exchange services for cryptocurrency include: Coinbase, Gemini, Binance.US, and Kraken. In choosing an exchange service, consider cash advance and buying fees, as well as location basis, since additional charges may apply for services being sent outside their native country. As for payment services, CashApp, Venmo, and Paypal are all trusted and can be used to exchange cryptocurrency. CashApp is a particular case as it offers something called "Bitcoin Boost" where users can earn Bitcoin by using their CashApp card for purchases.

Cryptocurrency exchange services are, however, it is not the only way someone can enter the market. Another common way to earn crypto is through investment brokers. Firms like Robinhood are commission-free and allow people to trade and invest.

Other ways that a person can buy crypto when starting out is through dedicated ATMs, crypto retail stores (for example, LibertyX, and CoinMap sell bitcoin), and direct transactions with another person.

It is, nevertheless, not always necessary to actually buy tokens with real-world money, although these methods do require more effort. There are numerous tasks that can be completed in order to earn cryptocurrency, as it is with any other salary-driven job. These are usually all within the digital realm, since this is where the coins are native. A couple examples will be described: Blockchain mining, gaming, and writing, although it is important to realize that these are just a few examples as more jobs are coming out that pay in crypto due to their nature.

The first example, blockchain mining, was already discussed in Chapter 1. It is when a person dedicates their computer space to hold and update a copy of the blockchain ledger of a specific cryptocurrency platform. In exchange for their service, they are rewarded with tokens. It is also important to keep in mind that mining is based on a Proof of Work (PoW) decentralisation model, and, as more new cryptocurrencies shift to different, more sustainable models, mining may become more and more irrelevant, and therefore it is important to do research on the models that are used by the cryptocurrencies in which you are investing. Regardless, to get into blockchain mining, a user must usually spend a couple thousand dollars on equipment, not to mention the electrical cost. The efficiency of the computer also plays a factor in how much money is earned, as faster computers will be able to mine quicker, earning more than average or slow computers. Just like investments, it is a gamble: Is the value of the currency going to be worth the costs involved to get started and to maintain the rig?

Another example of a cryptocurrency job is through blockchain gaming, which will be further expanded upon in Chapter 8. Last chapter, we discussed different games and apps that approach the metaverse, and many of these were built into the blockchain, allowing users to earn real cryptocurrency by playing games and/or selling goods on game-specific marketplaces. Though the profits can strongly vary and are also quite risky, it remains a solid and perhaps more inviting entry into the world of crypto trading.

Finally, there are some jobs that are employer-employee modeled in the digital world. One such example is online publishing companies which pay their writers to churn out articles about cryptocurrency, and then pay them in cryptocurrency.

Placing Your First Investment

Here we will be going through a step-by-step process to place your first couple of investments in cryptocurrencies, all depending on which cryptocurrencies you have decided to invest in, how you plan to divide your money, and how much money you plan to spend in total.

How Much Should You Invest?

The first thing that one must decide is how much money they are comfortable investing in such a volatile market as that of digital currency. Due to the particularly gamble-like nature of the industry, you should never invest more than you are willing to lose, and you should not rely on it to support you financially in any way. Other than wellness issues, investing too much money in crypto can also cloud the judgement of the individual, stressing them out and causing them to sell their shares if they see a sudden drop in price, which is a valid strategy as will be discussed later in this chapter, but not when it is done on impulse rather than by thorough thought.

Most experts follow the 5% rule: To never put over 5% of an investment portfolio into cryptocurrency. Ultimately the decision should be based on the individual's comfort level, and some young millionaires have made it by investing up to around 10% of their income despite the 5% rule. The main guideline nevertheless remains to never dig into money that provides for necessities in both the short and long term.

Finally, if an exchange service like Coinbase is being used to buy cryptocurrencies, keep in mind exchange fees that will be added on top of whatever investment is made. Transaction fees, deposit/withdrawal fees, trading fees, and escrow fees all may apply, and therefore should be taken into account when calculating how much money you are willing to put into the service.

Where To Invest?

In general, it is much safer to start out with some of the biggest cryptocurrency platforms, such as Bitcoin or Ethereum, because there is more certainty to their continued growth than fresh, new altcoins. However, although very risky, buying fresh, new altcoins would bring in the possibility of getting into a future popular market for cheap—that "I knew them before they were popular" type of feeling.

In the cryptocurrency portion of your investment portfolio, it is also important to not put all your eggs in one basket. This means that, with the budget cap that you have set in place for yourself, it is wise to divide your investments between a few different cryptocurrencies. In this way, it becomes possible to put in a bigger chunk of money into safer bets, and then invest a smaller amount that you are comfortable losing in a riskier marketplace, holding this as a longer-term investment.

"Stablecoins" are also an alternative that can be added in small amounts to your portfolio. These are low-value coins that are less volatile than altcoins or bitcoins because coins are created and destroyed to keep it at around the same value. There is controversy as to the usefulness of the coins, particularly because they have not shown any or much gain in the long-term for their investors. One of the most popular stablecoins is Tether, which has hardly ever surpassed the $1 USD mark in value.

Like in other investment markets, the idea of liquidity does apply and differs with different cryptocurrencies. The high-cap markets such as BTC or ETH are some of the most liquid coins in cryptocurrency because they are the most popular, thus most widely accepted by most companies. Because of this, it is easier to find exchange services or buyers willing to make the transactions for physical cash.

Liquidity is something to consider when choosing cryptocurrencies for your portfolio since coins with low liquidity will be difficult to get rid of if they are not working out.

So, how does one divide their investment budget based on all this knowledge? Well, often when starting out, people will divide their money between BTC and ETH, which are the two biggest and most established cryptocurrencies and thus fairly safe long-term bets in comparison with smaller altcoins. They are also the most liquid cryptocurrencies, meaning that they can be most easily cashed out whenever the investor desires. A common and simple diversified plan is simply 50% BTC - 50% ETH, which is a completely legitimate option to take. One way that is often used to create a crypto portfolio is to divide investments between high-market cap coins (BTC, ETH, etc.), medium-market cap coins (MATIC, BTT, etc.), and low-market cap coins (ATLAS, CGG, etc.). High-cap coins should make up the majority of the portfolio, say around 50-70%, since they are the lowest risk and are most likely to provide long-term gain. Mid-cap coins can make up another around 20-40% of the portfolio since they do come and go and are not so established, but if successful, can provide high ROI (Return on Investment). Next, low-cap coins should not account for more than 10% of the portfolio and are likely to be regularly switched around since these currencies have a high tendency to come and go, and are treated more as a "lottery," since, if one does shoot up in value, the ROI would be huge.

The cryptocurrency portfolio, again, also doesn't have to just include payment and utility coins like these ones either. Parts of the portfolio can also be taken up by stablecoins in small amounts in order to add liquidity, and NFTs, either on marketplaces or gaming platforms, although this will be discussed in more detail in Chapter 8.

To finish off, asset allocation also does not need to remain static forever. Depending on how market trends shift or just personal preference changes, the members of the portfolios as well as the percentages to which the budget is going towards, and even the amount of the budget itself can all be changed as time progresses, markets shift, and you feel more comfortable making decisions with this part of your money.

Waiting Out VS Conservative Investment

In general, trends show that younger investors tend to pick riskier trades, whereas older investors pick more conservative ones. The way the younger people view it, they have more time to "wait out the market," where they can wait longer for the cryptocurrencies in which they have invested to pick up above the price that they paid. Older folk tend to veer towards smaller successes, choosing cryptocurrency markets that are more likely to be cashed out for a higher selling price in the short term.

This is not simply just a question of age, though, and brings up a good consideration when choosing an investment strategy. You must ask yourself, when choosing each cryptocurrency as part of your investment portfolio: Do you want smaller, short term gain that is less volatile, or would you rather wait out the market for possible larger success? The issue is further complicated when one realizes that waiting out in shorter time frames, up to three months, results in more situations of net losses than waiting out over longer periods of time, say, around two years (Subburaj, 2021).

When to Buy

If you choose to buy your way into the cryptocurrency markets, there are a couple of things of which you must be aware. First, repeated continuously because of its utmost importance: crypto markets can vary as much as 20% within every day since they are extremely volatile. However, they are also incredibly difficult to predict, so even long-time, experienced investors cannot predict the perfect time to enter the markets.

One way of figuring out a market entry point is the Dollar Cost Averaging (DCA) strategy. This strategy consists of taking your money that you are looking to invest in a cryptocurrency and then dividing it. Each equal fraction is invested in intervals of time, regardless of the market price of that day. This way, once everything has been invested, the actual price that has been paid becomes the average of the cryptocurrency market price over this time frame, giving the investor a bit more security over their entry point. For example, if you are planning on buying 10 BTC, then you might decide to buy 2 BTC every Monday at 8 a.m. of every week for a month. Although some days you would be paying more than the previous one, it still gives some control to inevitable volatility. If DCA sounds familiar, it is perhaps because it follows the same logic as an SIP (Systematic Investment Plan) often used in the investment world beyond just cryptocurrency.

Following the DCA strategy also does not have to be followed to the letter. Since it can often be difficult to swallow paying an investment that is at a higher price than the previous week, what some people opt to do is reserve a portion, say, 20%, of their budget to add to investment days where the market price was lowered or that they think is the lowest of the month, therefore increasing opportunity to lower the average paid over the investment period.

Understanding market cycles can also be a key factor to understanding better entry points. Often, cryptocurrency markets will form bubbles of one or two years, where prices rise up and then fall back down, and the cycle repeats itself. Although this is not an exact measurement, it can serve as somewhat of a guide, and if the market seems to keep falling when you invest, it can provide some incentive to wait out the cycle. Following these trends from websites that track them, such as on CoinMarketCap or Google Finance can provide useful guides, but cannot be taken as an exact prediction for the future.

Cryptocurrency Wallets

All cryptocurrencies require their own "wallets," information storage centers, and these wallets cannot mix different currencies. Therefore, if you are carrying bitcoins, you must have a Bitcoin wallet, and if you are carrying Ether, then you must also have an Ethereum wallet. Each wallet contains a public and private key which should be kept secret from anyone but the owner, since the keys are what allow access to the cryptocurrency stored inside.

Wallets can be "hot" or "cold," and these are generally used with different purposes in mind. A hot wallet is one that is connected to the Internet. Because of this, transactions being paid in crypto can be done quickly and efficiently, yet since the private keys of the wallet are generated via the Internet, this type of wallet is more vulnerable to hacking, in which case the user risks losing everything. Within this category are also exchange wallets, which are provided by a seller who has the private key to it, to a buyer, who deposits the cash into it and then can no longer access it because they do not know the key.

Hot wallets often hold small, manageable amounts of cash and are primarily used for those who participate in many transactions. Some examples of exchange companies that allow holding hot wallets on their platform are Coinbase and Electrum.

Cold wallets are the opposite and are the main storage service for investors. These are more secure and harder to hack than hot wallets because they are kept on hard drives, paper, or other offline methods. In the case of paper, the private and public keys of the wallet would be printed on a piece of paper after the acquisition of the wallet from a website. That piece of paper can be stored either at a local bank through safety deposit boxes, or in safes within the owner's house—anything to keep it safe and secure, since it is the only way to access the record of the wallet other than the blockchain itself. The problem with both paper and hard drives is an obvious one, though: if the storage medium is lost, then the cash in the wallet is lost too. Some examples of trusted cold wallet companies are Ledger, which creates hardware devices, and TREZOR, which generates keys offline.

Apart from wallets, there are some services that decide to provide physical coins for the popular Bitcoin for a premium in order to cover manufacturing and shipping, however this can seem counterintuitive against the whole premise of cryptocurrency to cut out physical money.

There are some ways to offer further protection to your cryptocurrency wallet. The first is to keep all software up to date on a computer and often backup your cold wallet. Another way to prevent hacking is to use a multi-signature system to access the money. This means that the approval of a group of people is required to proceed through any transaction being made by the wallet, that way a single hacker controller cannot withdraw money.

In order to transfer money into the wallet, during every transaction, the wallet ID (address) that comes with it must be entered into a field, after which the cash can be transferred.

Setting a Target Return on Investment

Now that you have made your first investment into cryptocurrencies, you can set goals for each of them; target ROIs that, if the market reaches, you will be comfortable cashing out some of your coins. This solidifies an actual plan for the future of your money, regardless of how well the market seems to be doing at the time when the target is reached.

Of course, this is not a set rule. If you want to gamble more on your investment, you could always just wait it out over years and years until you feel like cashing out, however it does give a good guideline and allows you to better observe the market with a keener eye in the future.

When finding that the coin value has indeed reached the target ROI, the market's general tendency should also be observed, since if you are in a market cycle's "bubbling" phase, where it is either on the rise for the past months or on the decline, it will be easier to liquidate the assets.

Cashing Out

Now that you have made your investment and waited out the market for however long you have decided, whether three months or five years, you may want to cash out your crypto into the physical money of your country of residence. This can either occur because your target ROI has been reached and you want to take out some of the investment while you're ahead, or as a way of crystallizing your losses after you notice a continuous drop in value.

How Do I Cash Out My Crypto?

Cryptocurrency can be used to buy certain products, depending on the seller. Many large companies are beginning to accept currencies like Bitcoin for purchases, however, for many people, there is a better feeling to just sell crypto when it is possible to make a target ROI in physical currency, of which the value is much more stable and is also more widely used as of the current day and age.

There are a couple different ways to sell your cryptocurrencies. The first and simplest is through exchange services and hot wallets. On whichever exchange service for which you have signed up, there is usually an option to sell for cash, usually with certain transaction fees. For this reason, keep in mind how much money you are withdrawing and whether or not the fee is worth it. If it is not enough to justify the transaction, perhaps consider waiting the market out for longer to earn more cash that you feel comfortable withdrawing, or simply withdrawing more of the investment as it stands.

Peer-to-peer transactions also allow a return of physical currency for crypto. In this kind of deal, you are the one who chooses the price and the terms of the exchange. Usually, the return is an e-transfer.

For some of the bigger cryptocurrencies, ATMs have become a viable option, such as for BTC or ETH. These work just like bank ATMs, and are physical devices that must be found in your area. Transactions done this way are harder to trace and pay in physical cash but are dependent on location.

HODLers

Many investors stick to a "Hold On for Dear Life" strategy, known as HODLers. These people do not ever take out any of their investments in the hopes that after several years, the market will keep a general rising tendency. While this has resulted in some millionaires, it has also shown once-millionaires losing all their money as time went on, and has also shown people who never gained big through crypto, instead reflecting high loss percentages from their cryptocurrency portfolios.

This strategy is an incredibly risky one and it is recommended that new investors take a safer approach, knowing when to quit while they are ahead.

Crystallizing Your Losses

One reason that you may want to cash out your investment in a cryptocurrency is in order to "crystallize your losses." This happens when the exchange rate dips below around 60-70% losses on investment (Anuj, 2021). To crystallize the loss means to sell off the coins before any damage is done and then rework your portfolio accordingly. You may find that you do this quite often with the low-cap coins in which you invest, as these are the most volatile.

All-Time Highs

Before you start investing with cryptocurrency, you should be able to answer the question: why would someone buy coins from me when its exchange rate is at an all-time high? For many people, it would be better to wait until the crypto prices seem to have dropped recently and are now rising again in order to buy. Others may see the value steadily rising and want to get in early. Finally, there are those who may take the techniques about which were discussed in the "When To Buy" section of this chapter, where they may use a DCA strategy, where the actual price of the coin is irrelevant on that particular day, or are watching market cycles. Regardless, these are all considerations when timing a sale of some of your coins.

Careful With Your Cash

The world of cryptocurrency investment is a steep learning curve. In Chapter 10, you will find some common mistakes and misconceptions that people who have never invested before may have.

CHAPTER 8: MAKING MONEY FROM NFTS

Digging further in depth about choices of investments as well as amounts of dedicated cash towards them, there are certain specifics to keep in mind when sifting through non-fungible tokens. It was briefly mentioned in Chapter 7 the possibility of including NFT investments in your cryptocurrency portfolio, however, how do you do that if you are not an artist? Why do people buy and sell NFTs as opposed to physical or commissioned art?

What Gives A Digital Image Its Value?

Non-fungible tokens can take a couple different shapes and forms, but at their base they are simply images. So what's the craze? Well, the value of these NFTs is truly in the eye of the beholder, however, in this case, perhaps more like "beholders." Consumer interest in the product drives the price of it, and therefore generating millions of dollars to artists, who put out artwork that they have developed, popular brands or people, who take pictures that they believe people will find interesting enough to want part of its ownership, like the famous NFT made by the CEO of Twitter; a screenshot of his first tweet. They are also not confined to being 2D either. Buildings on the Decentraland gaming platform are also, for example, considered NFTs, simply for being a digital asset on this blockchain-programmed dapp. In the case of these buildings, placing them on the LAND owned by the buyer could increase that LAND's value, thus making the transaction profitable, and this in turn means that the building itself is valuable.

NFTs are different from regular commissioned or physical artwork because they must be completely unique with verifiable ownership. This means that, though technically an image of an NFT can simply be downloaded on anyone's computer with the PC's innate functions, the ownership of that NFT is definitively stored in the blockchain, and this is much harder to forge. The information that makes up the asset is stored here as metadata, and this is what is bought and sold by users, rather than the actual image itself, giving quantifiable proof of ownership that cannot be replicated by copying or screenshotting the art.

The tokens' value can somewhat be quantified by four components: utility, past owners, liquidity, and projected value (Chang, 2020). Two major categories of utility include game assets like buildings in Decentraland and tickets that can serve as entry into events. Another way that NFTs can provide utility is by sellers' partnerships with other companies, say, to offer discounts to owners of a specific token. In the future, it is projected that NFTs that have found a way to be interoperable through the metaverse between different platforms will shoot up in near immediate value.

Past owners will affect the value of a token because strong brands, popular figures, and influential people all attract large attention and thus a large consumer base to the products. Liquidity deals with the ease at which the NFT can be traded on secondary markets, and the higher the liquidity, the higher the value because people are attracted by the idea that it will be easier to sell than some other items. Finally, projected value increases current value for the simple reason that, if people believe they will be able to resell for more than they paid in the future, they are more likely to buy now.

Buying NFTs

How to Buy an NFT

In order to buy an NFT, one must first identify where they can be found. Because of their nature tightly related to blockchain programming, most commonly they can only be bought with utility cryptocurrencies, that is, ones that are native to crypto platforms that allow blockchain dapps. The biggest market of NFTs is, naturally, found on the biggest utility token platform, Ethereum, and thus uses ETH for sales. Solana, another example of a utility token platform, also is able to carry its own NFT marketplaces, and though not as developed as Ethereum, is fairly new and continues to grow, hosting more and more dapps.

On these platforms, there is not a singular place to find NFT marketplaces either. These can be strongly associated with dapps, meaning that one must go to these applications, and then be able to find marketplaces on some of them. In blockchain gaming networks in particular, there is almost always a marketplace tab where NFTs can be bought. There are also other marketplace hubs for dapps which can act like an online shopping website in nature, such as OpenSea, Rarible, or Foundation that are great websites for buying NFTs. Keep in mind that when using a hot wallet on an exchange service, there are withdrawal and transaction fees that are put in place when you are ready to buy.

The great part about having Ethereum established as a central hub for non-fungible tokens is because it is the oldest player of its kind in the game. All these images, assets, and tickets bought can be used anywhere else in the Ethereum space, although they cannot be used on other cryptocurrency platforms.

Furthermore, it is not always necessary to buy NFTs in order to get started in collecting them. Just like with acquiring cryptocurrency, doing certain jobs will grant the user unique NFTs that are highly liquefiable. For example, providing liquidity to some ETH exchange services like Uniswap, an ERC-721 token (LP-NFT) can be granted, which is basically an etch of some basic information on the user, the liquidity pool, and the value. This LP-NFT can be sold fairly easily afterwards on liquidity pools.

Once the NFT is bought, it ends up in your cryptocurrency wallet, and can be accessed from there.

Finding the Right Tokens to Buy

When buying NFTs with the purpose of selling them later on or using them to increase the value of other assets that you possess, there are certain strategies to keep in mind in order to choose the most promising ones in terms of consumer gain. It is first important to always have your end goal in mind: eventually gaining more money from the NFT than you paid. To this end, either you will eventually resell it off or you will earn passive income from it.

Foremost, you should be buying something you like. Because there is no guarantee that it will appreciate in price in the future—as with anything involving decentralized finance, or DeFi, the market is highly volatile and fairly unpredictable—you should get some enjoyment in the process at least.

Originality is also something that you must look out for. Many NFT artworks bandwagon off of popular and expensive pieces which have already known success, however these knockoffs rarely do so well. Looking for NFTs that stand out and concepts that have not been done before definitely increases the chance that it will go up in value and that you may predict a future trend within the community.

Moreover, checking sale history can sometimes give an indicator to the trends in the value of the artwork. If it has a track record of selling for higher than what it had been purchased for, it is possible that this will continue to be the case. However, the opposite can be true as it could depreciate in value as soon as you buy it , leaving you at a big loss. What can prevent to a certain degree unwise purchases is by setting a budget. This is the amount of money that you would be comfortable spending on an NFT and potentially losing if you cannot resell at a gain. Having an NFT collapse in value like this is yet another reason why you must buy something you personally like, because you may be stuck with it.

So, you have found an NFT that you like and think is original that also seems to have a good or neutral sale history (perhaps you are even the first buyer!). There are a few criteria by which you can then further vet the token to make sure it is a good purchase. The first is researching the artist themselves; what is their brand, their public image, and other projects? One may find copies of popular NFTs on marketplaces, usually screenshotted or saved and then reposted by scammers. Doing research on the creator of the NFT you are looking to buy will notify you if you are looking at a duplicate rather than an original. Next, you may observe the NFT's presence in the community, so check to see if in general, people seem to like it, and what are its criticisms. Finally, you can research the brand associated with the NFT. For example, if it is related to Axie

Infinity, you should be familiar with the game and know the demographic of people to which it could be resold.

All the above information applies when finding NFTs for price appreciation and eventual resale. However, what about the other option of passive income? This is done by fees associated with using the NFT to further the value of something else. In the realm of the metaverse, this could look like charging a fee for a viewing of an art museum filled with collected NFTs. In blockchain gaming, the example of buying a building NFT and placing it on Decentraland LAND to increase its value also applies.

Selling and Reselling NFTs

NFTs can take the form of any image or visual asset, whether 3D or 2D, objectively beautiful or not, and even objectively interesting or not. For this reason, anyone regardless of who they are has the option of creating NFTs, and yet even if a person is not the creator of artworks, they can still profit off of the industry by resale of ones that have been previously purchased.

If creating NFTs, the creation, minting, and publishing processes are all important to understand. The main sources of income generated by these images should also be discussed. If buying and then reselling NFTs, one should be familiar with the resale process and the restrictions in terms of their ownership over that artwork.

Creating, Minting, and Selling Your Own NFTs

First of all, NFTs can be created out of anything. They can be actual art that can attract buyers because of its aesthetic, originality, and wit, or they can be photographs or screenshots, depicting something monumental, strange, relevant, or nostalgic. An NFT can even take on the form of a video, audio file, text, collectibles, or non-digital items like real estate. Anything that is completely unique (non-fungible) can pretty much sell as an NFT, however when choosing a format, it must be able to be uploaded onto a marketplace platform. Most of all, creativity is the most important factor for common marketplaces.

Once a format and an idea is chosen and the token is created, it is time for it to be minted, meaning it goes from a simple file to an NFT. Minting refers to the process by which the token is added onto the blockchain, locking it in indefinitely as an NFT on the market. A royalty clause is also added by the owner of the file when the NFT is put into the blockchain, which stipulates resale royalties that can be earned as passive income after subsequent owners pass it on.

In order to mint your NFT, you must have a cryptocurrency wallet ready which can hold the currency used on whatever marketplace you choose to publish it. An example from earlier in the chapter, you may recall, includes OpenSea. There is a one-time fee associated with the minting process. Once you sign up for the marketplace of your choice, you can mint it there, and after giving some information on the piece, it is added to the blockchain, and officially minted and published. This is, however, not the end of your side of the process. There are gas fees, transaction expenses to account for the processing energy needed, that are associated with first making the NFT available to sell, and whether you will allow the sale to happen as an auction or as a first-come-first-buy status. Processing a sale, gifting NFTs, cancelling listings or bids, and minting a same file on multiple marketplaces all require additional gas fees, which is why it is important to weigh the risk of publishing something. You should ask yourself if the process is worth this fee.

Many serious artists and NFT creators will bypass the whole marketplace and create their own website, where they sell their tokens on a strictly primary market between creator and buyer.

Once the minting process is done and the NFT is officially on a website, it can be viewed by anyone and thus sold to anyone interested.

Ownership Restrictions

To understand what exactly it is that you own when you buy an NFT, you must understand what is being changed in the blockchain. To refresh your memory: the metadata of an asset is stored on the blockchain, and that metadata contains all the information pertaining to the asset. It is also what is being bought and sold, rather than, for example, a picture itself. This metadata that is being passed around is what is referred to as a "token," which clarifies the name of the NFT: it is a "non-fungible," completely unique, and non-exchangeable with other assets. The "token" metadata confirms ownership on the blockchain for the specific asset being sold. Because all that is being passed around is the token of the asset, the buyer is only granted access to *some* of the digital record, and the original asset is still that of the original creator.

First, the token cannot be duplicated. This keeps the rarity and the uniqueness of the NFT which is what allows its opportunity to rise or decline in value. If there is a duplicate found online, then this is most likely a scam.

Other rules related to specific NFTs are outlined in smart contracts, outlining terms, and conditions laid out by the creators. These act as licenses and are dependent on the artist and the specific token at hand. They will list activities for which the NFT can be freely used, and those for which it cannot.

The main rights of the buyer include: ownership of the NFT by digital or physical transfer, access to the NFT source file, and rights to resell the NFT and keep a portion of the deposit.

Nevertheless, when it comes to the original creator, intellectual property rights are given, making copyright theft illegal. This means that any new buyers cannot make the NFT available to everyone and cannot adapt the asset or file in any way. The buyer also cannot sue anyone based on the NFT. Of course, all of these issues should be outlined in the terms and conditions before buying that token.

Resale of Purchased NFTs

According to the ownership rights of the NFT buyer, they are allowed to resell the token. This resale again transfers the metadata of the original asset, though the original asset still remains under the copyright of the creator. In this way, though, all sales and resales of that NFT are recorded in the blockchain and the prices for which they sold is forever embedded there.

In order to resell an NFT, it can be withdrawn from your cryptocurrency wallet and listed on marketplaces, just as any other token, whether new or not. In this case, it would be referred to as a secondary market.

Most of the time, when reselling an NFT, most of the sale price goes to you, the reseller. Royalties are applied to that price that are given to the original creator of the asset, making it a source of passive income for them.

Receiving Tokens From Gaming

The use of non-fungible tokens in blockchain video games is considered by many to be not only their future, but the future of gaming, and of technology as we know it. These projects are the most complicated and thus most ambitious, since there is much more than just art that goes into making these NFTs—they have to be functional in-game. NFTs have already been incorporated in games like Axie Infinity or Space Atlas, where the marketplaces and economies are already established.

The interesting part about NFTs in games is that it is not always necessary to buy them before having to resell them again. To clarify, in a game like Space Atlas, NFTs can be found and foraged throughout the world, and the finders gain ownership of them simply for having picked them up. They are then allowed to resell them at their own will, just like any other NFT or any other marketplace. To a lesser extent, a game like Axie Infinity does the same thing, where although one might buy an NFT of an axie, this axie can be bred by the player to create new axies that are owned by them and thus can be sold as their own assets.

CHAPTER 9: INVESTING IN METAVERSE OPPORTUNITIES

One of the biggest up-and-coming opportunities to make money in crypto investments is, of course, through the metaverse. In this chapter, you will learn concrete strategies to make money from blockchain gaming, and investments in augmented reality and everything else "metaverse." First, you will learn how to decide in which areas to invest and then how to divide those investments smartly, not only in different platforms but in different NFTs or other resources within each platform.

Making Money From Gaming

Blockchain gaming has a large role to play in the upcoming metaverse and is already one of the largest industries within the current state of the platform. It utilizes a bunch of elements that are already the aspiration of the metaverse such as decentralized game-specific economies, sometimes a certain measure of interoperability, and most importantly a connection to NFTs.

In order to make money from blockchain video games, the ways in which their economies work must be identified. Although they will run on a crypto platform that uses a certain type of currency, such as Ethereum with ETH, these games will add another layer of complication and have their own in-game currencies, such as MANA in Decentraland or SAND in The Sandbox. The difference between these in-game cashes and their parent currencies will also be discussed.

Play-To-Earn

The concept of "play-to-earn" is one that will come up a lot when learning about money-making from blockchain gaming. These games will use this idea as incentive for players to keep coming back. What is meant by play-to-earn is the decentralization of a program, along with the exchange of all its assets and identity, which leads to the formation of fully-fledged economies, in which a player can get rewards from the completion of in-game tasks that then either lend themselves to real cryptocurrency or can be sold for such. This is allowed to happen because every reward earned while playing actually has its ownership transferred to the player in the form of an NFT.

NFTs

In most blockchain play-to-earn games, rewards take the form of NFTs rather than direct to cryptocurrencies. This further allows user flexibility, since they can go and sell that NFT anywhere they want and for their own prices and terms, regardless of whether that marketplace is connected to the gaming platform or not.

Finding or purchasing the right NFTs is largely dependent on the game at hand. Some games, like Axie Infinity, require a knowledge of the different stats of an axie as well as how well the offspring after breeding could fare on the marketplace, that is, if selling axies is the goal. On a game like Decentraland, the goal would be to develop the piece of LAND NFT that you would purchase with other NFTs, such as buildings, in order to increase its value either for resale, rent out space by playing landlord, or charging an entrance fee for those wanting to visit. Not only would you have to keep in mind how certain NFTs would increase the value of the LAND, but at a more fundamental level you should consider the location of the LAND you are buying. Busier areas like at the heart of cities will be more expensive for a smaller plot because they are more desirable.

From this, it can be deduced that there are a couple of different ways to get NFTs from a game. The first is, of course, by purchasing them through the game's native marketplace. Sometimes some elements of the game can be purchased elsewhere, such as the sale of specific gamer tag names for Decentraland on OpenSea. Other game elements that could be purchased from a game's native marketplace include avatars, buildings, props, clothing, items, and RPG weapons.

Another way to get NFTs from gaming is through exploration and foraging. In Space Atlas, for example, the world can be explored and certain items can be discovered where the ownership of the NFTs is given to the player. These can then be sold through marketplaces.

Other methods in which NFTs and cryptocurrency can be earned will, nevertheless, be dependent on the game at hand. For example, in Axie Infinity, the player battles in PvE and PvP to earn rewards, but can also farm items and potions which can also all be sold for cryptocurrency.

Governance and Utility Tokens

As should be well known at this point, cryptocurrency technology has a common name, like Bitcoin or Ethereum, as well as a name for their coins, which in the case of this example would be bitcoins (BTC) and ether (ETH). However, going beyond coins, cryptocurrencies also make use of tokens that make use of the main coin and can be applied in similar ways, the difference being that the token is much more specialized to a particular use on the platform. For example, Ethereum, which calls its different tokens under the umbrella term "ERC20," hosts ATLAS tokens from the game Star Atlas. These tokens are specifically designed for its in-game purchases, but cannot be used outside of the game until they are converted to ETH. Another example of tokens are NFTs. These tokens are specifically designed for the of appeal of their uniqueness, more of an entertainment and perhaps aesthetic value. By these two examples, it becomes clear that there are different types of tokens, and these are thus categorized.

Although there are many different categories for tokens, a couple of the main types in gaming are utility and governance types. Utility tokens like ATLAS are designed for a future use. They are the most common in-game currency, as is the case with ATLAS in Star Atlas. Utility tokens are not used as investment tokens for ROI, and instead their value does not go beyond their programmed use.

Governance tokens, for example POLIS from Star Atlas, are a little bit different. Rather than having a future use at which time they can be expended, they hold voting power towards game updates and developments, and have been built for the main purpose of keeping a game decentralized despite still having clear creators and developers. Using governance tokens, game proposals can be voted upon or even created. These tokens can also do more than just cast voting power. First, they can be used for stakes, meaning a fixed interest rate is placed on the tokens and then set to rest over a couple of years before being returned with the interest applied. The crypto over this time is used to support the game on the blockchain. Another way they can be used is for loan creation, and also for yield farming methods, where cryptocurrency is put to work in order to generate more cryptocurrency. Yield farming is quite similar to staking crypto, except it is more tied up into liquidity pools.

Investing in a Game

To get started investing in a blockchain game, usually a game will have some of its native tokens for sale. AXS in Axie Infinity and SAND in The Sandbox, for example. These tokens can usually be bought from different exchange services. Recall that these are the services on which you would hold hot wallets, withdraw and exchange money for various cryptocurrencies.

Choosing the right game in which to invest is dependent on two main factors: risk-tolerance and enjoyment. The first factor involves how risky you will allow your investment to be. In popular, established games like Axie Infinity or Decentraland, the risk is quite low, meaning although ROI may be smaller than riskier games, they are a safer bet. This does not mean that these safer games will automatically grant you high returns, but that it is less likely. Less popular up-and-coming games are of higher risk, and, just like how crypto coin investments work, high risk either has the potential for high ROI or terrible loss. An example of a newer game that is high risk but has potential to have a boom in popularity is Star Atlas. This game, built on the Solana blockchain, plans to be one of the first AAA crypto games, meaning high-quality graphics and a large open world. This also means, though, that it will be in its developmental stages for a long time. In order to keep attention and to build up its value as well as the value of its tokens, it releases in stages, therefore players can even join right now if they wanted, and there is already a community for them despite limited functionality of the game itself.

The second factor on which game choice depends is enjoyment. The main purpose of any video game is simple entertainment value to its player base. Though these new crypto games have play-to-earn potential, largely tied to their appeal, you should not be investing in a game you simply do not like, since, in the long run, you will be involved in it if you keep putting money in it.

In the end, just like with direct cryptocurrencies, you will not be choosing just one game token or one blockchain game in which to invest. Rather, from the portion of your cryptocurrency portfolio, made in Chapter 7, that you have perhaps dedicated to blockchain games, you can make a completely new gaming portfolio, where you can separate your investments between many different gaming tokens. In this way, you can spread out over safer tokens and riskier ones, and can also explore more games that interest you.

How to Invest in Augmented Reality

Since most augmented reality companies are not yet heavily involved in the crypto side of the metaverse, we will divert and discuss stock opportunities and strategies in relation to AR technology. We have talked about a cryptocurrency portfolio, and how much of your general investment portfolio this should constitute from Chapter 7. Stock investments are the part of this portfolio that will likely have some of the highest returns if allocated correctly, and especially now, with the metaverse emerging in full force, there is great opportunity towards jumping on the bandwagon.

When building an investment portfolio, there are generally a couple of main categories: Stocks, bonds, mutual funds, real estate, and cryptocurrency. Cryptocurrency, being the most volatile market, is advised to only constitute a short portion of the portfolio, around 5% or lower. Stocks are the next riskiest market, either being able to generate high ROI or causing you to lose all that you have put into it. Risk profile, which is how willing you are to risk your money, will determine what percentage of the portfolio goes into stocks, and this is usually in conjunction with bonds—20% is generally considered low risk, whereas up to 80% is considered high risk and an aggressive profile. Bonds serve as a stabilizer to the risk of stocks and crypto, stabilizing the value of the portfolio, which is why if one were to put little investment in stocks, they would likely increase their bond investments, and vice versa.

General trends show more conservative investing strategies among older people, as they cannot wait out the market as long as younger people who are perhaps saving for retirement. This brings up the idea of a time horizon. Before choosing where to invest and the risk levels of the various companies, stocks, and bonds, you should decide your time horizon just as you had when considering which cryptocurrencies to invest in. Therefore, if you have a smaller time horizon, having a low-risk portfolio is more suitable, and if you have a larger time horizon, you may consider if you are comfortable with a more aggressive yet smart portfolio.

Augmented Reality Stocks

AR and VR stocks are still new, having been introduced during the past decade or so. Yet in that time, they have generated billions of dollars and are on the rise with the sudden boom in popularity of the metaverse in the wake of Facebook's rebrand to Meta. Safer stock options for AR and metaverse companies are often the biggest ones, like Meta, Alphabet (Google's parent company), or Apple. All of these companies are working towards VR, like Meta's acquisition of Oculus VR, or AR, like Google's ARCore, or Apple's Apple Glasses. Riskier stocks would be for new projects, perhaps made by companies that are smaller and lesser known, yet based on market trends, the direction of the metaverse, consumer interest, and just personal faith in the product, you may find that there is high potential for ROI.

CHAPTER 10: RISK AND REWARD

We have been quite optimistic about investments in the metaverse and its future, however, like everything worth doing, it does not come without risk. We will thus in this section cover some things to look out for during the process, and some common mistakes with first-time investors, as well as how to avoid them.

Tips on Investments

Purchase Automation

Purchase automation is a feature of many exchange services that allows a person to automate transactions on a regular basis. Therefore, one could set up the service to spend a set amount of fiat cash, fiat meaning that it is issued by the government like USD or CAD, every month on a certain cryptocurrency. Thus, regardless of the current price of it, you would be paying the same amount and therefore just getting different quantities.

The appeal of purchase automation is that it lessens the stress of finding a good time to enter a market, and resembles in some ways the Dollar Cost Averaging (DCA) strategy discussed in Chapter 7, but on a larger time frame. It is also hands-off, meaning you do not have to stay on top of your timing.

Copy Trading

Copy trading is another technique used by beginners and consists of copying the investment trends of more experienced users. This does not—and in some ways *should not*—mean allocating 100% of your investments to do exactly as the professional does, but rather can be a means of further diversifying your cryptocurrency portfolio. If, say, you allocate 10% of your money into copy trading, then this could give some more stability to your portfolio. On the occasion that your other investments do poorly, perhaps the other investor that is being copied could have fared better with their currency choices, and vice versa, if they did badly, then you still have the rest of your portfolio which could recuperate losses.

The way which copy trading works is via websites like eToro or Coinmatics, which allows users to link their wallets to an experienced investor of the user's choice, and then copying trades will be done automatically and in real time by the site. When choosing one of these investors to copy, some factors to consider are the same as when building the rest of your portfolio, such as risk tolerance and diversification of past investments, and others must be taken to verify credibility, such as number of past followers and general reputation.

Staking Coins

The idea of staking coins has already been discussed within the context of blockchain game tokens. Staking can be done, however, in some dapps not associated with gaming as well. If you only plan to buy and hold onto your coins with the intention of watching their value increase, then this is a good strategy for some of them. However, if you plan to make purchases using crypto or plan to use them in other ways, then it is not so good as it locks your coins into the platform and provides interest on them, often between 5% and 25% over a certain amount of time.

Risks associated with staking, however, include a lack of regulation and of code vetting for flaws in some dapps. This means that, when coins are staked to these organizations, there could be the possibility of hacking and of losing all the funds, which is why it is important to do research on the dapp in which you plan to stake your coins and also be wary of the risk.

Hedging Crypto Trades

Hedging is a more advanced crypto investment strategy that consists of predictions of future market trends. The investor then places two trades based on what they predict, and traditionally place it in a 60/40 ratio. First, they place an investment towards what they think will happen to the market as a primary trade, and then they take action for the exact opposite so that, in case they are wrong with their primary trade, this secondary trade can recuperate some of the loss.

In cryptocurrency, primary and secondary trades take the form of "going long" and "going short." Going long means that you are buying cryptocurrency at a price you believe will rise in the future, and therefore you are paying less than what you plan to make from that crypto investment. Going short is the opposite:

you predict that the exchange rate of your crypto will fall, and therefore you sell it before the market has the opportunity to put you at a loss. In the context of hedging, therefore, your primary trade could be to go long and your secondary trade could be going short, or vice versa.

This is a very risky strategy in which to partake and thus should be used in moderation. The reason it is so risky is because it opens up a possibility that, although there can be large ROI and coverage of losses from it, an investor could end up paying *more* than what they originally invested, going below even on it.

Stop Loss Orders

A stop-loss order can be put in place on an exchange service connected to your wallet in order to lower some of the risk of cryptocurrency investments. It dictates a price, called the stop price, of the investor's choice at which time their funds are locked into the market until the exchange rate of the cryptocurrency reaches it, and must be cancelled manually otherwise. Stop loss orders can allow the buying and selling of coins only once the stop price is reached. It can also have the function of automatically exiting the market when the stop price is reached in order to avoid losses.

Being Careful

When first entering into the world of the metaverse AR/VR, cryptocurrencies, NFTs, and blockchain gaming, overeagerness, though good for spirit, can often lead to clouded decisions. Being careful of where your money is going, and never taking any of it for granted is the key to smart investment and may be the difference between losing everything and becoming a crypto millionaire.

Timing

First of all, trying to find the perfect timing to enter a market is a common mistake for beginner cryptocurrency investors. The truth is that there is no perfect time to make an investment and that even professionals struggle to predict it because of its insane volatility.

It can seem like buying crypto when the prices are really low is always a good idea, since it shows a large opportunity for growth. However, some cryptocurrencies will not rise just because of your investment, and instead will just fall steeper and steeper until you're forced to crystallize your losses. Even though a price looks good one day does not give much indication for what will happen in the future, which is why educated guesses based on market cycles and previous trends are made as a gamble, and you should not place all your faith on perfect timing.

"Easy Money"

Cryptocurrency is far from being "easy money." It must be treated as an educated gamble by investors because, considering its decentralized nature and the amount of competitors that keep evolving in terms of technology and efficiency, the market is and probably always will be extremely volatile and unpredictable. The golden rule is, of course, to *never* spend money that you need elsewhere and only spend what you are comfortable losing. As far as "easy money" goes, anything that you make can disappear just as fast, so you must be constantly on top of your earnings, making it not-so-easy money.

Crypto Investment Scams

As with anything else involving money, and particularly in the realm of cryptocurrency because of its lack of regulations as of a result of its decentralized nature, there are many scams and false opportunities out there, of which the traps can be well-disguised to the eyes of the inexperienced.

First, there is the fake coin scam. Buying these coins gives the opportunity for criminals to steal your identity and your money, as well as installing spyware on your computer that they can use for phishing. In order to prevent this, you must properly research all the coins in which you plan to invest and make sure they are legitimate.

Second, there are wallets out there, lesser known and sometimes with anonymous creators, that are attached to purposely faulty software. This software can be designed to allow the creator to hack in and access your money. Another scam related to wallets is the promise of free cryptocurrency by emails or texts as part of an ad for the scammers' wallet software. These wallets are not legitimate and should be avoided.

Finally, with some small cryptocurrencies, some people will buy large shares or get them by pre-mining before their release to market and thus have some influence over price fluctuation. They can then make the price either rise or drop, and, during these drops, will fake-sell their coins. They'll begin the transaction with an investor just to cancel it and take off with the money.

In general, the best way to avoid any scams is to be prudent and do thorough research on whatever cryptocurrency or wallets you are planning to get, where it is coming from, and the seller's reputation, as well as general opinion and reviews.

Watch the Market—Don't Forget About Your Crypto!

It is easy to forget about your cryptocurrency after it has been purchased, since there is no physical reminder of it lying on your countertop or beside your bed at night like a physical wallet. However, although you may be sitting on this money for a long time before it is time to cash out, it is important to keep track of it.

For one thing, if you do keep a cold wallet outside of an exchange service, make sure to keep its keys in a safe location and do not lose or forget them. Losing the keys to the wallet means losing access to everything inside of it, as it cannot be accessed without them and these keys can also not be shared with anyone, just like the PIN of a bank card.

Keeping track of the market and the exchange rates of your crypto investments as they shift is also vital. Even if you are no longer actively investing, since in a period where you perhaps reach your target ROI or you see that the market is falling and you need to crystallize your losses, you may want to try and liquidate rather than watching the opportunity pass by. That being said, you should not be overly stressed out about market prices dropping or not being able to sell your crypto right away. If you do find that you are so stressed about losing the investment that it is beginning to affect you, then you may have invested too much money into it and should withdraw until you are investing with an amount that you are fully comfortable losing if it doesn't work out.

Finally, many people, even those very successful, get into the "hold on for dear life" mindset discussed in Chapter 7. In your own investments, remember that the end goal is to make money that you can actually use. Sometimes, even if it's just a portion of the investment, you must know when to begin cashing some of that money out, rather than prolonging the wait ever longer in order to maximize ROI. It's a continuous gamble and the longer you wait with everything in there, the more precarious that money can become. This does not mean that it is bad to keep money in cryptocurrency over long periods of time, but that it is not a bad idea to occasionally cash a portion of that money out into a safer, less volatile fiat coin.

CONCLUSION

The metaverse is coming whether people like it or not. With it will come a revolution of cryptocurrency, NFTs, particularly in relation to blockchain games and decentralized applications (dapps), and augmented or virtual reality technology. With Facebook's rebrand to Meta in November 2021, people who have never heard of the metaverse have now been sucked into it, and this widespread acknowledgement of its impending integration into society's digital lives all across the world has given crypto investors, who have experience with the metaverse technology that already exists, a golden opportunity to profit off of it.

The future of cryptocurrency is full integration into the mainstream metaverse, and becoming truly accepted as a valid payment method. As it is with NFTs, efforts will be taken to abolish myths about decentralization that may scare some people away from change and to abolish proof-of-work mining in favour of other, 100% clean-energy, proofs to verify blockchain technology.

Mark Zuckerberg, the CEO of Facebook, stands to play a key role in leading the metaverse revolution thanks to his huge platform and enormity of funds, as well as all his personal investment in the project. As for the already-established metaverse, more people will come to know about them and begin playing blockchain games, operating on a play-to-earn basis, and regularly using AR and VR technology, offering the benefits of full immersive experiences that would aid in numerous aspects of society such as education and healthcare.

Though the metaverse does present some social risk like addiction and privacy and safety issues, environmental risk in the shift to clean energy, and technological challenges in terms of receiving funds, creating innovative and immersive experiences, and finding what users like to use, there is still so much time for it to develop, and the support that it receives gives hope that the risks and challenges can be well-managed.

From its beginnings through a concept of a virtual world in a novel, the metaverse has already come a long way. Some games use metaverse-like technology without calling themselves "metaverse," whereas others, a mix of blockchain games that provide monetary reward for playing and regular video games that have approached digital social connections in an AR/VR environment, have done so long before Meta's rebirth labeled themselves metaverse.

When it comes to investing in cryptocurrency, NFTs, and blockchain gaming, the golden rule is to never spend more than what you are comfortable losing because of the extreme volatility of these decentralized markets. Aspects of investment like diversifying your portfolio and knowing when to cash out are all important to remember. Finally, always vet everything in which you plan to buy or invest in order to avoid falling for scams that are rampant in crypto particularly due to the lack of moderation that comes from a decentralized platform.

Cryptocurrency is such an exciting opportunity, particularly in relation to metaverse technology towards which the future of the Internet is headed. The volatility and nature of the markets discussed, and as it is with any financial industry, makes it impossible to take any advice as a certainty for success. The best is to start small, invest smart, and do not be discouraged by failure.

www.ingramcontent.com/pod-product-compliance
Lightning Source LLC
LaVergne TN
LVHW022320200926
848481LV00004B/1379
* 9 7 8 1 8 0 7 6 5 1 1 2 1 *